XMAS 2009

HAPPY XMAS DAD

LOTS of LOVE

DAVID ALISON

GAYLE & ANDREW

GRANDSLAM

How Ireland achieved rugby greatness
– in the players' own words

Alan English with the Ireland team

Photographs by Billy Stickland and Inpho

PENGUIN IRELAND

Published by the Penguin Group
Penguin Ireland, 25 St Stephen's Green, Dublin 2, Ireland
(a division of Penguin Books Ltd)
Penguin Books Ltd, 80 Strand, London WC2R ORL, England
Penguin Group (USA) Inc., 375 Hudson Street, New York, New York 10014, USA
Penguin Group (Australia), 250 Camberwell Road,
Camberwell, Victoria 3124, Australia (a division of Pearson Australia Group Pty Ltd)
Penguin Group (Canada), 90 Eglinton Avenue East, Suite 700, Toronto, Ontario, Canada M4P 2Y3
(a division of Pearson Penguin Canada Inc.)
Penguin Books India Pvt Ltd, 11 Community Centre,
Panchsheel Park, New Delhi – 110 017, India
Penguin Group (NZ), 67 Apollo Drive, Rosedale, North Shore 0632, New Zealand
(a division of Pearson New Zealand Ltd)
Penguin Books (South Africa) (Pty) Ltd, 24 Sturdee Avenue,
Rosebank, Johannesburg 2196, South Africa
Penguin Books Ltd, Registered Offices: 80 Strand, London WC2R ORL, England

www.penguin.com

First published 2009
1

Copyright © Alan English, 2009
Photographs copyright © INPHO Sports Photography

The moral right of the author has been asserted

Set in Quadraat, Aachen and Impact
Typeset by Smith & Gilmour, London
Printed and bound by Firmengruppe APPL, aprinta druck, Wemding, Germany

A CIP catalogue record for this book is available from the British Library

ISBN: 978–1–844–88221–2

CONTENTS

PROLOGUE
KIDNEY CALLING

Killiney, County Dublin, 16 March 2009

Ireland's Grand Slam decider against Wales in Cardiff was still five days away, but for some of those in camp at the team's hotel it was an anxious afternoon. The side to face the Welsh would be named in the evening and made public the following day. Declan Kidney, the head coach, had shaken his squad the previous week by making four changes for the defeat of Scotland at Murrayfield. It was a violation of convention, of the belief that when the stakes are rising you stick with a winning team. For years, that had been the way the Ireland rugby team worked. But Kidney trusted his instincts and set off a controlled explosive. All of a sudden, those who had started the first three matches on the bench could allow themselves to hope.

RORY BEST: It was the biggest game of all our lives. It was the one we all badly wanted to start. We had tried to keep a lid on any Grand Slam talk, but it was unavoidable at that stage – it was everywhere. Some guys could feel confident about their places and some of us were just hoping.

This is how it works when you're not in the team. You get to Monday afternoon or early evening and the phone rings. The screen flashes and you see the name you don't want to see: Declan Kidney. For a second you think, 'I wonder if I don't answer this and ignore him till tomorrow will he pick me?' But then you answer and he says, 'Would you mind calling around?'

The call normally comes an hour before dinner, around five o'clock. Your heart sinks. But we're all competitive people, so a little part of you thinks, 'Hold on. Maybe he's ringing to tell me the game plan, to tell me that I'm starting.' So you

LEFT: Jamie Heaslip was one of four members of the starting XV who were dropped for the Scotland game – and sweated before Declan Kidney's selection for the Grand Slam decider

try to kid yourself a bit. But you know, deep down, that it's not going to be good news. You go to his room and he's very good. He tells you exactly how it is and where you stand. As a player, all you can ask for is honesty. But it doesn't make it any easier to take.

I had been picked for the Scotland match and I was happy with how I'd played. So yes, I was hopeful. As it got closer to the team meeting, I looked at my phone a few times. *Don't ring me. Please.*

TOMMY BOWE: Four players were dropped for the Scotland game and it fairly scared the wits out of the rest of us. Geordan Murphy had been out of this world at training, carving us apart on his own. So I was thinking, 'Jesus, he'll probably be given a go next.'

BRIAN O'DRISCOLL: Declan had spoken to me about what his changes were. I'm not [involved] in the decision-making process and I don't know how things would have been if I had objected massively to one of the decisions. Maybe I'll never know if I have any leeway. But you've got to trust your coach. People say that coaching at that level only goes so far, that it's about the players – but you still really rely on what your coaches have to say and what they have to offer. So I was accepting of his decisions. I had spoken to one of the Munster boys and he had expected changes [against Scotland]. Sure enough, there were four. Declan made a good point – why should you wait for a defeat to change things? I liked the idea of trying to build the squad. If you're missing one of your key players, the only way other guys will be able to play at that level is if they have the experience.

PADDY WALLACE: Declan had never talked about a Grand Slam. He likes to give the opposition respect. But after the Scotland game there was no hiding from it. There was a Grand Slam on the line against Wales and if there was ever a match you wanted to start in in your career, this was it.

BRIAN O'DRISCOLL: From 2004, when we won the first Triple Crown, I was thinking, 'We can win the Slam here, if we get our act together.' That was why I wanted to give the captaincy one last shot. It would have killed me to have captained the team for six years and then, the year I give it up, we win the Slam. I wanted it

badly. It was massive for me. I hadn't had success like the Munster boys had with their two European Cups.

GERT SMAL, FORWARDS COACH: Big players – and there are a couple on the Irish team – need to taste some big success along the line, to make their playing careers worthwhile and satisfying.

PAUL McNAUGHTON, MANAGER: As a nation we haven't had players as good as O'Connell, O'Driscoll and O'Gara on the same team. The team had been around for five or six years. As a player myself, I went back to a time in the Seventies and Eighties when winning a Triple Crown was fantastic – and nearly impossible. It would have been a travesty if the most experienced players in this team hadn't won a Grand Slam. I don't think there was a team over the past forty years outstandingly good enough to win it – outside of this group. A team can't just jump up and win the Grand Slam from nowhere – it doesn't come around for one year. So this was a good team. And when all these guys retire, it could be a long

time before you get that much talent on the field again. They had done well over a period and then failed miserably in the World Cup. They were good enough to win a Grand Slam – and they hadn't done it. So the way I was looking at it was, they'd better bloody well win it now.

TOMMY BOWE: From day one, the Welsh game was the one I wanted to be involved in, because of my teammates at Ospreys. I was thinking, 'I want to play in that and I'd love to have a stormer.' It was the most nervous I'd ever been before a team selection. The guys dropped the week before hadn't played badly. I've set standards for myself and against Scotland I didn't reach them. I made mistakes. If Declan wanted to drop people, well …

PAUL O'CONNELL: Competition for places is brilliant for any team. Against Scotland you had four guys coming in, playing to keep Ireland in the hunt for a Grand Slam and playing for a shot at starting a Grand Slam decider if we won. Four of the hungriest men you could possibly have. And then, coming off the bench, you

had four equally hungry men. Then you had the rest of the team, slightly on edge. So I thought it was a good thing.

DECLAN KIDNEY: I didn't like leaving anybody out, but we'd said we wanted to build a squad. When do you do it? There is no right time. Every time you make a selection call, in my job, it affects a person. To me, that is important. You've affected his life.

The four fellas who started against Scotland deserved to. Geordan was playing well – maybe he should have started too. It wasn't to be smart, to say they needed a kick up the pants. There was nothing wrong with anybody's work ethic. I don't think I can explain it, other than to say: experience. We were after playing three games, so maybe throw something in. Analysis gets thrown a little bit. But even there, I have branched into something – as if that was the reason. It wasn't – it just felt right. That doesn't mean it was right. But it felt right.

TOMMY BOWE: I chatted to my mum and dad on the phone on the Sunday night. They told me a lot of people were heading to Cardiff. I started to feel a bit uneasy and they sensed I was worried about my place. Later that night, my mum was putting on a wash. She wanted to have dad's lucky jumper ready in good time. She took it out of the machine and there was a stain on the front of it. So then she started thinking, 'Oh Jesus – that's a bad sign!' She put it back in the wash before she went to bed. She said to herself, 'If that stain comes out it, it'll be a good sign for Tommy. And if it doesn't …'

She and dad were tossing and turning all night, worried about my place. The next morning she was up at cock-crow, shot downstairs and took the jumper back out of the washing machine. The stain was gone. We're not a superstitious family but that day they were looking for lucky socks, clumps of clover, horseshoes …

JAMIE HEASLIP: Not being involved in the Grand Slam game would have left me feeling short-changed by the whole thing. Deccie, he's always going on about honesty. So when he dropped me against Scotland I let him know how I felt. He said he wanted to reward the guys for training well and playing well with their provinces. I told him I wasn't happy with his decision. I had my reasons: basically, I was on form. This is nothing against Leams, because Leams is a quality player.

DENIS LEAMY: I sat down with Deccie after the second or third game and he said, 'Look, the lads are playing well.' Sometimes you've got to hold your hand up and accept it. I agreed with him. I didn't think any of them deserved to be dropped. My gut feeling when I was picked for the Scotland match was, 'No matter how well I do, I'll be surprised if I stay in.' That's just being honest. As it turned out, I injured my shoulder and I had a fight on my hands just to make the bench.

JERRY FLANNERY: Rory works hard on his game. The more I see him working hard, the harder I want to work on my game. It's so close between us and when you're not in a team you want to know why. You're always trying to nail a coach down. 'Why aren't you picking me?' You want them to give you a specific reason, to say something like, 'Your tackle count isn't high enough.' Because if they say that, then you can go and make twelve tackles at the weekend: 'Now my tackle count is higher – pick me.' But they never do that. Never. You just don't get a coach who gets caught like that. It's a bit of a merry-go-round. You ask questions. They shimmy. They avoid the questions.

DECLAN KIDNEY: You can't really give them a reason why they are out. I remember telling one or two of them that. I said, 'If I was to tell you a reason why you are out, I'd be trying to justify my decision. I'm not going to try and do that. This guy has been going well. We're trying to build a squad and he deserves a go.' If fellas don't see there's an opportunity to get in, how can you keep encouraging them to keep going?

JERRY FLANNERY: The thing is, you're not going to play rugby your whole life so you need to be as greedy as you can. I told Declan, 'I desperately want to win a championship, a Grand Slam. You not selecting me, you're putting what I want into someone else's hands. I can't directly affect it.'

I tried to play around, in my head, what Declan was trying to do. I tried to work it out. My argument was, 'If you as a coach pick me, I have a responsibility to you to do my job. When I do my job well and we win, I think you have a responsibility to pick me again.' I thought that's how it worked. And when he dropped me I thought, 'There's no real guarantee of getting your jersey, even when you do play well.'

DECLAN KIDNEY: Jerry's response was completely rational. You can only agree to that. But you have to say, 'Look, this is *my* point of view.' And he didn't walk out saying I was being irrational. Every player wants to play every minute of every match. Ask any player who has ever been substituted if he minded – he won't even answer. He will give you a look that says, 'What do *you* think?'

JERRY FLANNERY: Myself and Tomás O'Leary went into Dundrum Shopping Centre the day after the Scotland game. Rory and Strings had both played well. We were saying, 'I can't believe we got this far in the championship on the team – now we're dropped and the two lads have had good games.' We went off and bought a load of stuff to cheer ourselves up. My head was all over the place. I bought some crappy books and jeans that would have fitted Paul O'Connell – 34-inch leg. It was Depressionville in our room.

TOMMY BOWE: I was so nervous, but I didn't want to show it. I went down to breakfast and I walked past Deccie. I was holding my breath and thinking,

'I'm going to get the tap here.' He had a look at me, but I was chatting to somebody by then. So I thought, 'Jesus! He just looked at me! Is this it?' I tried to avoid him then. Crazy stuff goes through your head. I thought, 'If I see him coming again, I'll sprint to the other end of the room. If he can't get hold of me before the meeting he won't be able to drop me. I'll sit down, everybody else will come into the team room and I'll be safe.'

JERRY FLANNERY: When it's a tight decision, everything matters. Every single thing you do in training. In those moments, so close to the team selection, you think, 'This could tip it my way – if I do this well here.' We went out to do some lineout throwing but I had hurt my shoulder before the Scotland game and I hadn't taken any anti-inflammatories that morning. So I couldn't throw. Rory had to do all the lineouts. I could feel it slipping away from me.

That's it, I've just made the decision easy for them. It's gone. I'm out.

RORY BEST: Jerry was still struggling a small bit with his shoulder, so yes, I was half thinking, 'They'll go with me here, because of his shoulder and because of the way I played against Scotland.'

JERRY FLANNERY: I went back and the doc gave me some painkillers. They kicked in and I was able to do a weights session and do it well.

RORY BEST: Monday evening, the phone rings. I look at the screen. It says, 'Declan Kidney'. Straight away you get that sinking feeling.

Oh God. Here it comes.

'Could you call in, Rory?'

'Right. Okay.'

As I was walking to his room, I saw Denis. We were rooming together. A week ago, when he picked the team to play to Scotland, we were just so happy. It was obvious Denis had just been in before me. We both knew what was happening. There were no words, just a look. I knew he wasn't walking away from Declan's room having been told he was starting. He knew I wasn't going to Declan's room for a social visit.

Declan opened the door and looked at me.

DECLAN KIDNEY: I hate telling people they're being dropped – I absolutely hate it. For a player, it can be a feeling of utter rejection: 'I'm being dropped. I've been shafted. I'm out.'

RORY BEST: From the look on his face, I knew what was coming. Being honest, I'd known from the minute he rang me. I spoke first.

'I presume it's not good news?'

He said, 'Look, I'm sorry, I don't have a start for you.' It was by far the shortest meeting myself and Declan had over selection for that Six Nations. And it was far and away the most disappointed I've felt about a team selection. I didn't really say a whole pile.

PADDY WALLACE: How did he announce it to me? God, I've blocked it out of my memory, it was so traumatic. No, I had a missed call from Declan and a message on my answerphone. It was, 'Can you come and see me?' I rang him back. Couldn't get hold of him. I had a shower, came back out, and there was another missed call from him. I called again and he said, 'Paddy, can you come and see me in my room?'

A million things are going on in your head on your way to his room. There weren't too many words spoken. He just said, 'I'm going to go with Gordon.'

When he told me I said, 'Declan, I'm gutted. I'm totally gutted, but I respect your decision and I'll back Gordon up 100 per cent.' It really hurts you, because you want it so much. You have to let it sink in and then try to get your head right for the next day.

JERRY FLANNERY: I sat down in the team meeting a little bit broken. I hadn't been told anything, but you never know with Declan. I was still thinking, 'I've lost my chance here.' Next minute he started announcing the team …

'Marcus Horan, Jerry Flannery …'

Oh my God. Happy days. Suddenly the week has a whole new meaning. You can't celebrate being picked – it's only 5 per cent of it. But now you have the chance to go and do your job. It's not getting the chance that kills you.

TOMMY BOWE: When it was announced the first text went to mum and dad. Just two words before I slipped the phone back in my bag.

I'm in.

It was a happy day for us as a family. I was just so glad to be back in the team, after being dropped, after not being selected for the World Cup. There was a fear that if I got dropped for this one, what a disaster. I was rooming with Paddy. All the guys dropped for the Scotland match had gotten back in – except Paddy. I was so happy for myself, but devastated for him.

DECLAN KIDNEY: Did they deserve to be dropped, three of them? Did Paddy deserve not being brought back in? No. I don't care if it takes four seconds or four hours – they deserve their time if they are getting bad news. You block away time, insofar as you can. You don't always get it right and there's no easy way of giving bad news.

The only good thing about that side of this job, compared to the provincial one, is that I'm not telling fellas whether they have contracts or not. That's the only thing that's worse. You have guys in front of you that you think an awful lot of – as people and as players – and you're telling them you don't have a start for them. If there's one part of the job I could get rid of, that would be it.

GORDON D'ARCY: Getting back in the team – it was why you do all those hill runs, lift all those weights, make the sacrifices. It makes it all worthwhile. I know Paddy quite well, so it's hard. He had done so well up to that. But at the same time I wanted to play – so it's hard to find a balance there between the two emotions.

There are a lot of people in the same boat. Shane Horgan, Mal O'Kelly, Girvan Dempsey, guys I've been so close to for so many years. It was tough for them too, not being involved. He could quite easily have gone with Paddy. I didn't have my all-time best game against Scotland, but I probably just did enough to put a bit of doubt and thought in his head: 'Maybe this guy might be able to do something.' And that's all you can do.

RORY BEST: The following day was Tuesday. In match weeks, you have the option of spending Tuesday night at home. Normally, I'd hang around but this week was different. I just needed to get out of camp and get away. I went home.

TOMÁS O'LEARY: I was really pissed off when I wasn't selected for the Scotland match, but I had to stay positive and not bring down the morale of the group. Before that match there was a fear that you won't get back in – and then Peter had a brilliant game, so I was nervous. Training with Peter has made me push myself harder and I was relieved to get back in. It was tough on Peter, but we all have those emotions when we don't get picked. You have to be selfish.

PETER STRINGER: I put myself in there, I gave myself a chance. I was happy in myself, knowing that I'd done well against Scotland. After that, it was up to the coach to make his decision. It would have been great to start the Wales game, but not getting picked would have been a whole lot worse if I'd screwed things up against Scotland. I would have felt really bad about that.

Tomás and me were friends before and I'd say we're even closer buddies now. There's good respect there.

JERRY FLANNERY: We did media on the Tuesday. Charlie Mulqueen [*Irish Examiner* journalist] was saying to me, 'You must be feeling massive pressure.'

'Not really, Charlie ...'

'But it's been sixty-one years since Ireland won a Grand Slam! This could be an unbelievable achievement – you have to be feeling the pressure.'

I wasn't. Not then. It was only when we got down to the Thursday that Rog and Paulie were saying, 'You're not going to grasp how big this is, because there hasn't been enough time for you to take it all in. But it's going to be one of the biggest things you've ever done and you've got to pull out all the stops if we're going to win this.'

Rugby is probably what I do best, so I don't see a point in getting nervous. I try to put my head in the best possible place. When we got to Cardiff, people coming over from Ireland were saying, 'You have to win this Grand Slam. You're on the brink of making history.' Eighteen months before that, we were being slaughtered by the media. The team had been built up so much before the World Cup – and then panned at it. There was an awful lot of criticism – stuff about people's personal lives. There was way more of that than I'd ever seen before. And now this. It was some turnaround in eighteen months.

CHAPTER 1
NEW ERA, NEW IDEAS

On the evening of 19 March 2008, Eddie O'Sullivan sent a text message to Ireland squad members – as well as certain rugby writers – informing them that his resignation as Ireland coach after six and a half years was about to be made public. The official announcement came later that night, after a severance settlement had been negotiated by his representatives. Among his players there was a widespread view that O'Sullivan's departure had become inevitable. They had performed poorly in the Six Nations, and wretchedly at the World Cup the previous autumn.

Three Triple Crowns had made O'Sullivan the most successful and the most powerful coach in Irish rugby history, but the team's failure at the World Cup was comprehensive and traumatic. O'Sullivan, protected by a four-year contract, battled on to the Six Nations but his team had lost its way badly. He had long been a controlling figure, uncomfortable with delegating. At their best, his teams were characterized by verve and backline brilliance. For some time, however, there had been unease among key members of the squad – in particular the Munster forwards – over his belief system and the game plan he insisted upon.

O'Sullivan had his Triple Crowns for vindication, but more than anyone he knew a Grand Slam had vastly more currency. He craved a Slam, but equally he needed to win it his way. That meant he wanted to go around teams – and not through them. The kind of psychological and physical warfare – pack on pack – that had made Munster European champions was not his way.

He wanted power plays, intricately worked overlaps, training-ground tries that were audacious in conception and execution. That did not sit well with his forwards and they came to feel marginalized and frustrated. If they attempted

to impose their physicality on a team and got knocked back, there would be a rebuke from the head coach. They would have seen the setback as temporary, a small battle lost amid a war in which psychology was everything. But, when it came down to it, O'Sullivan did not have enough appetite for the kind of destruction they wanted to bring about. There were other frustrations. His absolute faith in and focus on his front-line players could leave others feeling excluded and unwanted.

While the team was winning with tries from the so-called golden generation of Irish backs his authority and philosophy were beyond question. But the World Cup changed everything. The confidence that coursed through his team when they demolished England at Croke Park six months before the World Cup was gone.

TOMMY BOWE: I didn't get picked for the World Cup, but for more than a year after it guys were talking about how they were still recovering from it. There was a very serious hangover.

STEPHEN FERRIS: It was tough at the World Cup. When the team's not doing well, you think a couple of changes would bring a bit of life to the squad. Eddie always thought the same squad would come good in the end. It never did.

DENIS LEAMY: Eddie brought that team a long way from where it started, but by his own admission, things had got a bit stale.

MARCUS HORAN: Eddie did a lot for us and we won a lot under him. But sometimes these things run their course and no matter how much effort you put into it, you hit a wall. That's what happened.

JERRY FLANNERY: Putting bodies on the line is one of the strengths of the Munster pack but it was never fully utilized at national level before. If you do something well every week for Munster, then you come to Ireland and you're not allowed do it, you feel: 'I'm not being given a chance to show what I can do here.'

PAUL O'CONNELL: We had spent a lot of time trying to run around teams with Ireland. We probably hadn't used the forwards enough to create space for the backs. We

were a backs-orientated team and we had a good backline but we had to start taking teams on up front if we were going to be more successful.

First and foremost you have to take on the other team's pack to win rugby matches. We didn't always do that. Sometimes we would play teams with weak defenders in their pack or at ten and we would still try to go around them. They would just chase us out to the touchline and tackle us out there.

We used to play a wide-wide pattern where we would go from one side of the pitch to the other with two or three long passes, and while it worked sometimes, it probably didn't work enough. A lot of the game plans we tried under Eddie made us better players, improved our knowledge of the game and made us think. For me, it crystallized what I thought worked and what didn't.

RORY BEST: Come the pressure of an international, in the last ten minutes of both halves, you need a little bit less thinking time and a little bit more just challenging yourself mentally – and challenging them physically. Do you think you're able to get around this corner? Do you think you're able to get yourself off the ground to run twenty metres to get to where you need to be?

DENIS LEAMY: There was a feeling that we had one of the best backlines in the world and we could beat teams with power plays. The World Cup was a case in point. We'd go out and practise power plays, one after another. In training, we'd run through the defence and score nearly every time off these plays. But in a game it's different. You've got to put phases together, to dominate teams. When you dominate, the space does arrive out wide and then you can go there.

We were trying to go wide off first- and second-phase ball. We'd get a lineout just inside our own half and decide we'd try to bust them straight off with decoy runners. It was great in theory. It looked really well in training. But when it came to the heat of the battle it wasn't ever going to work. We never got that much control over the opposition.

DONNCHA O'CALLAGHAN: I found Eddie brilliant – I came on so much as a player under him. I love patterns, structure, accountability. When the shit hits the fan, you can tell guys, 'You should have been there, *you* should have been here and

> ❝ **Putting bodies on the line is one of the strengths of the Munster pack but it was never fully utilized at national level before.** ❞

you didn't fulfil your role either.' We're lucky we have an honest bunch because if you don't and you leave it up to the players you can get guys hiding.

It's about trying to get a balance of both approaches, I think. I've talked to Paul about this, I've said it to Fla [Jerry Flannery]. It's nearly an ongoing row. Of course I love it when we as forwards drive things, but sometimes you've got to look at the bigger picture and Eddie's wide-wide patterns resulted in us winning some big matches. It does mean you are splitting your pack a bit – and to be fair we do like to hunt together – but I just think the accountability factor is massive. It's grand for fellas like Jerry and Paulie because you know they're not going to be lost. Someone like myself, I prefer to have a bit more shape and direction, so there's no grey area. You can't say, 'I was going around the corner to carry that ball', because everyone knows your role is to hit that ruck at the first or second breakdown.

They slag me about that. They call me Johnny Robot. Leamy has another one – he calls me Johnny Notepad. He'll say, 'Hold on there now – give Donncha time to write this down and work it out.'

MERVYN MURPHY, PERFORMANCE ANALYST: Eddie liked to run it tightly. That's the way Eddie is and that's the way it was. He still had the coaches doing various things, but at the end of the day Eddie really had the say on everything. But it's hard to say that's the difference between us winning a Slam and not winning one, because we were close to winning a Grand Slam with Eddie.

BRIAN O'DRISCOLL: I would have the utmost respect for Eddie. I actually have nothing negative to say about him. I think he did a brilliant job for us for a lot of years: he brought our team on in leaps and bounds. The one thing I would say about him is he tried to take on too much himself and not delegate. He put

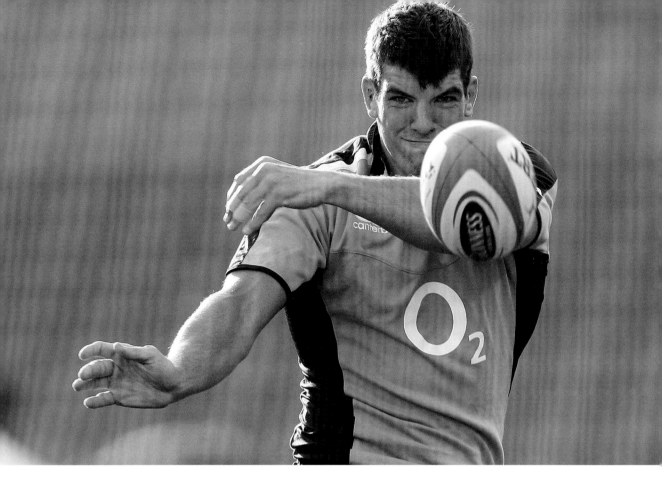

too much on himself at times. There were times when he tried to lease parts out to different coaches but I don't think he felt comfortable with that and then essentially it came back to him. That's where he felt at his strongest.

I don't think the World Cup was Eddie's fault. Okay, we got it wrong in the build-up to it. We weren't match-hardy. We didn't get playing rugby nearly early enough, we should have been playing rugby three or four weeks before we did.

You look back and think maybe we should have changed it a bit more in the tournament. That's all well and good – hindsight is a beautiful thing. We could have won the [2007] championship except for that last-minute try by France, so why wouldn't you stick with the guts of that team for the World Cup? They've proven themselves in the Six Nations championship, so why wouldn't you stick with them?

RORY BEST: I wasn't a hundred per cent sure what needed to change but personally I felt that a lot of the enjoyment of playing for Ireland and being involved in the Ireland squad had gone out of it. It was just a matter of how you got that back.

It wasn't something you felt would happen overnight.

GERRY THORNLEY, *IRISH TIMES,* 8 MAY 2008: When Declan Kidney informed the Munster squad at their meeting before yesterday morning's training session that he would be the new Irish head coach, his announcement was greeted with a huge round of applause. On what must have been an emotional day for the 48-year-old on reaching the pinnacle of his career, that would have privately pleased him no end.

DECLAN KIDNEY: Munster wasn't an easy job to leave, but I was always challenging the players to be as good as they could be and for me that was the deciding factor. I had left the Leinster job so that I could be closer to home. With the Ireland job, if you are prudent with your time, you can reduce it to one or two nights a week away from home. With Leinster it was six nights a week – there's a substantial difference.

PAUL MCNAUGHTON: I worked with Declan at Leinster, but unlike other people I didn't become emotionally distracted by his departure. I was used to working in business, where people left banks for different reasons – money, ambition, personal reasons. It became very personal, as if nobody has the right to give up a rugby job and go elsewhere. We all moved on. Five years later, after Eddie O'Sullivan resigned, the IRFU approached me about doing an Irish manager's job. I said it depended on who the new coach was going to be. When they eventually decided to give the job to Declan, they asked him about an acceptable person to work with him. They were happy, he was happy. So it happened. No reflection on anybody who was there assisting Eddie, but it was accepted by everybody that new faces were required all around.

On 24 May 2008, in Declan Kidney's swan song as coach, Munster became champions of Europe for the second time in three years. The victory – built on the back of a dominant pack, each of whose members was an Ireland international – suggested what Ireland might achieve under Kidney.

DECLAN KIDNEY: Once the Munster job was over, within two or three days you just want to get into the next one, because time is of the essence to try and put a team together. Niallo [Niall O'Donovan, former forwards coach] was going to be a hard act to follow. It needed to be somebody with experience who carried a bit of clout. As part of the discussion process that went on with the IRFU I was asked, if I was thinking of doing it, who would I be thinking of? I said Gert Smal was somebody I would like to meet. He'd been forwards coach for the Springboks when they won the World Cup the year before.

GERT SMAL: After the World Cup, I wanted a head coach position. I had applied for the Munster job, but around the same time the IRFU approached me to come for an interview. As it turned out, the two interviews were on the same day, in hotels right next door to one another in Ballsbridge. I went in and straight away I walked into Declan. I'd read a lot about Munster on the plane over and I recognized him from the newspapers. We started chatting. I hadn't wanted an assistant coach job again, but in my interview they asked me if I would help Declan as forwards coach. He had struck a chord with me immediately, so I was thinking, 'This could be the best way to get my foot in the door, get some experience of European rugby.' It was agreed that I would come back and meet with Declan again, spend a day with him.

DECLAN KIDNEY: A week later Gert flew into Cork. The day just seemed to fly. He's a very honest guy, there are no agendas with him. His track record in coaching the Springbok forwards was superb. He had also been a head coach and I got a real sense that he knew what the head coach needs as back-up. That came through very quickly.

GERT SMAL: We talked through our philosophies, the way we think about the game. How did he want to play it? I had a list of questions. We didn't agree on everything, but I think that's where the stimulation comes in, when somebody thinks a little bit different than you. He came over as very honest and genuine, which is what he is. We knew we wanted to work together. We shook hands on it. Declan likes to take long walks at night-time. I went with him once and I said to him, 'The way the whole thing happened, it was like it was meant to be for me to come here.'

RORY BEST: Once Gert was appointed I Googled him. You read the stuff in the paper but it does no harm to have a quick look yourself, to see if you can find out exactly what he's all about.

WWW.KEO.CO.ZA: Sources close to Smal confirmed he had no option but to seek employment elsewhere. Smal had big plans to work with black players in the Eastern Cape where he aimed to develop the next generation of South African forwards. This proposal was sent to SA Rugby in January, but after five months, Smal is yet to receive a response. Failure to keep Smal in the South African system is yet another blunder by the rugby authorities.

GERT SMAL: I started my career at provincial level in the Eastern Cape and I know the complexities, the politics and how to put it together there. There's a huge amount of passion for the game and the black community there is close to my heart. I wanted to share my experience and I put a proposal together for Jonathan Stones, who was MD of SA Rugby. He never came back to me. When I was flying

from Cape Town to London on my way over to my interview in Ireland, he walked into me in the business lounge. He was apologetic. He said he'd been busy with other things. On the flight from London to Dublin, the president of SA Rugby, Oregan Hoskins, was sitting two seats in front of me, on his way to an IRB meeting. There was a seat open next to me and he came back and joined me. He's a very good man. I asked if he'd seen my proposal. He didn't know anything about it. He was very cheesed off and he said I must forward it to him. But by then it was too late.

DECLAN KIDNEY: If the IRFU had wanted me to go on the summer tour [to New Zealand and Australia], I would have done. But it was their decision that I should start after it. There was even a discussion on whether I should go out or not. But that was one I took. Paul McNaughton and I used that opportunity to meet up with a few people over there. We had a list of names and I liked a lot of what I'd heard about Les Kiss. Waratahs got to the Super 14 final on the back of the best defensive record in the league. Les made a huge commitment to fly in from Japan to see us. That said 40 or 50 per cent of it for me. If a man is willing to do that, it's a good sign.

LES KISS: We threw questions at each other for a few hours. They said, 'We've been talking to a very prominent forwards coach.' They couldn't say then who it was but I saw a name I recognized on the corner of a sheet of paper: 'Gert'. I thought, 'There's only one Gert in the world – that I know of anyway.' I had worked with him before, so that made it even more attractive.

DECLAN KIDNEY: We went for lunch and we were able to chat away – about rugby, about other things. Sometimes you get on with people, sometimes you don't. The chemistry is vital because the defence coach does the job – it's the person you work with. The chemistry of the backroom team is just as important as the chemistry of the team – and it can be reflective of it.

On their way back home, Kidney and McNaughton met with Mark Tainton in London. Tainton had been Ireland kicking coach for six years, until the end of the 2008 Six Nations. He accepted the offer of a quick return. Alan Gaffney, who had replaced Kidney as Munster coach in 2002, was already on his way back to Irish rugby as backs coach for Leinster following two seasons at Saracens. Kidney and McNaughton felt he could perform the backs job with Ireland as well. After some initial misgivings, the union agreed. Mervyn Murphy, performance analyst under both Warren Gatland and Eddie O'Sullivan, completed the senior line-up.

There were other priorities. O'Sullivan had had an uneasy relationship with the provinces. Kidney was determined to keep them onside. But it had to cut both ways.

> **We threw questions at each other for a few hours. They said, 'We've been talking to a very prominent forwards coach.'**

PAUL MCNAUGHTON: A programme was put in place with provinces over resting players, making sure the international squad didn't play too many games. It was argued long and hard with the provinces and it worked reasonably well.

GEORDAN MURPHY: After Declan took over he came over to London and had a meeting with the players based in England. For the boys here the fear is 'out of sight, out of mind'. Declan said he didn't mind us playing over here – he was just looking to pick the best players. That was really refreshing, a nice way for him to start. I didn't enjoy the World Cup experience. After it, I thought about retiring from international rugby, but you're a long time retired and I love playing for Ireland.

LES KISS: Gert and I did a fair few miles early on. Those six weeks were all about getting the lie of the land, finding out what types of relationships we could forge in the provinces. My primary area is defence. It would be remiss not to say that when I got here there were certain good qualities. I've got a system, a different

‘ **After Declan took over he came over to London and had a meeting with the players based in England. For the boys here the fear is 'out of sight, out of mind'.** ’

way of operating. Each province worked a different system, different variations of line speed. Declan opened up the book and had a very democratic approach. To have a table where we could all throw things in was a really interesting process. Declan opened up this world. In doing that, he allowed us to find out about each other. There was a good sense of trust in those early meetings. You could throw things up without being judged.

MERVYN MURPHY: Some meetings went on for five or six hours, but I didn't notice the time going by. Maybe I'm being a complete rugby nerd, but I was having so much fun.

DECLAN KIDNEY: Just because meetings go on for hours on end doesn't mean they are good ones, but one sentence out of one of the six of us might be the difference between something working or not.

ALAN GAFFNEY: I did regard them as being a drag early on, but I did also understand that they had to be long. A lot of it was trying to lay down the basics of where we were coming from, what individual coaches perceived and wanted. I didn't think they had to be as long as what they were – but as time went on the meetings were streamlined enormously.

GERT SMAL: We as a coaching staff had to feel out each other as well. You can be a little bit sensitive in the beginning to each other's feelings. But ultimately what you want is for the head coach to have his dreams realized – the way *he* wants to play the game. Eventually he will have the final say. But when you have different

cultures, different people, different experiences, you're not going to bring it all together straight away. It doesn't work that way. Through my whole coaching career it has never worked like that.

The global trial of rugby's Experimental Law Variations began on 1 August: another challenge for the new coaching team. Four days later, forty players turned up to a four-day training camp in Cork, the first under Kidney.

GERT SMAL: Passion for forward play is part of Irish rugby as well as South African rugby, so it wasn't a huge change of thinking. That's where it starts, that's where you get the field position from. With all respect, what they did in the past was good. But I think they wanted some new ideas, they wanted to be a little more stimulated. Players can become stale at a certain stage, they need more stimulation and they were ready for that, for different ideas.

JERRY FLANNERY: Gert was difficult to get a read on at the start. He's not an overly chatty man. But rugby people are the same all over the world, and the more he spoke about rugby the more you got a feel for what kind of a fella he was. You could see he's a very passionate man. If he was playing, you'd like him on your team.

PAUL O'CONNELL: When you meet him first time he doesn't break down the barriers with an easy smile. It'll be a while before he smiles. He's actually got a very good sense of humour, but when you meet him initially there won't be many jokes. He commands immediate respect because he's quite a serious guy.

GERT SMAL: There was a learning curve for me. After practice in South Africa, we would go in a huddle, the same as before a game. I tried to do it with these guys after a scrum session. They all looked at me: 'What?! A huddle? *Now?*' So I just left it. It was something I had to get used to. They have different ways of doing things. They don't greet each other in the mornings. That was quite strange to me. I mean you don't have to shake his hand but at least say, 'Good morning', when you go into the breakfast room. Maybe they're just not good morning people.

DONNCHA O'CALLAGHAN: He came down to breakfast and he was saying to everyone, 'Morning! Morning! Good morning!' We were all looking at him thinking, *'Good morning? Just shut up and sit down! It's too early for you to be like this – it's not like we're not going to see you for the rest of the day.'* It was the same thing with the New Zealanders at Munster. They come in and they're giving high fives first thing in the morning and saying, 'How are *you*?' Ask John Hayes how he is before eleven o'clock and see what answer you get.

PAUL O'CONNELL: Sometimes we're a bit suspicious that we're not doing the right thing and the southern hemisphere are a jump ahead. But when Gert came in it confirmed to me that the sort of stuff we were doing with Niallo was really good. You have the professional guys in Ireland who have managed to figure a few bits and pieces out, and we're doing it, whereas in the southern hemisphere they have figured it out and they have terminology which makes it easier to explain. After a lineout he might say, 'You've got to chase his inside hip there.' We would have been doing that under Niallo, but not had the terminology.

DONNCHA O'CALLAGHAN: We'd catch O'Connell and Gert walking down the corridor together and he'd know he was in for it. He'd dread us seeing them together, because we'd started calling them father and son. They played a game of table tennis and Tommy Bowe made a massive fuss, got everyone in the room to watch the father and son battle. Who won? Ah, who always wins? Paulie shaded it. Thank God – it would have been a miserable week if he hadn't.

PAUL O'CONNELL: Most of us are clever enough to decide whether we want to bring new ideas into our games or not. We're the ones playing the game but you need someone – an ideas man – all the time, all the time. And then the strong personalities in the team can argue it or the young guys can say, 'Look, what about this?' If you have confident ideas and confident suggestions coming at you, it's great.

For every lineout session he always had a scrum-half for us to deliver to – be it Paddy O'Reilly the bagman or Dave Revins the masseur. It was something we had been quite poor at. Every time we didn't get it right you'd hear him roaring, 'Deliver!'

GERT SMAL: I'd done a fair amount of analysis on Paul, but obviously I didn't know him as a person. He's really something special, I think. We plan a lot together. It's important that we both understand the way each of us is thinking. He must feel comfortable and give confidence to the players around him, so what we put together must complement the team.

‘Some meetings went on for five or six hours, but I didn't notice the time going by. Maybe I'm being a complete rugby nerd, but I was having so much fun.’

English isn't my first language and when somebody asked me about him I said he was a machine. But in real terms, he's a quality man. If you go to war, he's one of the first guys you take with you. There are a couple of other guys and it's a pity that they are nearer the end of their careers than the start. Some of that pack, I wish I could have had my hands on them a couple of years ago. Like John Hayes. A special man as well. He gives the people around him a lot of confidence. So honest, not the loudest, but never shies away from any work. I enjoy the work ethic of the whole pack.

JAMIE HEASLIP: When it came to lineouts, the detail Gert went into was unbelievable. I was blown away – we all were. Even Paulie, I think – and lineouts are his bread and butter. Gert took it to a new level. When you see that commitment, you don't want to let the chap down.

DAVID WALLACE: He was very particular in the way he wanted you to stand at the back of a lineout, which way he wanted your foot to go. And when he says it, you take notice. You don't want to mess it up. He's a bit like Paul in that way.

JERRY FLANNERY: For Gert, it's all about timing, about shaving everything down to be at its most efficient. The scrum-half doesn't wind up the pass, like in the old days – he zips it. In a lineout, the ball has to shoot straight from the hooker's hands, without any backward spring. He would say, 'You can win all your lineouts, but if your delivery isn't right, you can't use the ball.'

At that camp in August, he was telling Paul that Ali Williams likes a particular type of jump: 'You've got to watch this, Paul.' And I was thinking, 'We're not playing the All Blacks for another three or four months – and he's thinking about it already.'

GERT SMAL: Lineouts are not just about winning the ball. From the second it leaves the hooker's hands, until you hit the contact, it's about how far you get over the advantage line. The beauty of the game is that the positions are very interdependent. It's about the hooker putting it on the spot, the explosiveness of the jumper off the ground, the accuracy and the timing of the players helping him to get that ball, the delivery of the ball to the scrum-half, the accuracy of scrum-half's pass to the fly-half or whoever goes over the advantage line, the speed they run into or through contact. And the philosophy is not to just run into contact, you run to go and score tries. You're not just running to set up another phase. The quicker you can score from any phase, the better. And the better the skill, the better the chances to score from first phase.

The scrum is also a place where a pack can show its unity, but certain basics must be in place. We could have a three-hour discussion on front-row play alone. There's a huge amount of time that must be invested. I'm still not happy about our scrummaging. I took a good look at them before I got here. I knew that suggesting just a couple of things would improve the scrum and that's all I could do at that stage. The next stage is to improve tactically a bit more.

LES KISS: You never know if you're totally prepared when you do a presentation to a new group of players, quality talent in a nation that isn't yours. But I had been through that with the Springboks and all I could do was make sure that my heart and my passion came through. I had to make sure that this whole thing was about building something worthwhile together. It wasn't just about stopping the opposition. It was about being a living and breathing animal, surging and hunting for opportunities.

Defence is a world of decision-making. To me it should be seamless and operate with everything else. The mindset has to be one of opportunity. What can we see? Where can we hurt the opposition? What are we smelling? It's a hunter mindset. Hunting for opportunity to change the game, to shift the game, to shape it, to get off the line, to send shooters opening up this world so that we're not just saying, 'Let's stop them.' It's about a willingness to get back up and put yourself where you need to be. That means no logs [players lying on the ground]. They really piss me off. Just get off the ground, don't be a log. If someone can't embrace that, it doesn't sit well with me. I was accepted well, but anyone can present something. The real battle is when you have to get out on the pitch.

MERVYN MURPHY: The guys were massively impressed with Les. He's a gentle guy who delivers his message brilliantly and clearly. The one thing you need in a defence coach is clarity. You need to be 100 per cent on it, bullet-proof. And that clarity is priceless.

> '**When it came to lineouts, the detail Gert went into was unbelievable. I was blown away – we all were. Even Paulie, I think – and lineouts are his bread and butter.** '

BRIAN O'DRISCOLL: It's really important that there is no grey area in defence. Les brought new techniques and it's so refreshing as a player to see someone coming in with new ideas. You think you've heard a hell of a lot in ten years but when you hear something new it gives you a hunger to defend better, to slow the ball up and choke the opposition.

LES KISS: We want to hurt the opposition. It's about utilizing the laws, about finding a way to have more impact in the tackle zone, once you've entered it, right through to the back end. And I think it made a difference. A lot of defence work is about how you make a tackle and get them to deck. I know every defence coach might say the same, but this I think has a different edge to it. But it only has an edge if it's believed in. From one to fifteen, everyone must feel that down in one corner of your jersey there's a little number seven on your back. Everyone must have a seven mentality.

DECLAN KIDNEY: I looked at the group and they were being bracketed as being over the hill, some of them. But they weren't. They had an amount of knowledge. We had some discussions – and discussions have to start somewhere. With us, they started with the four team leaders. We asked the players who they thought would represent them best. Sometimes, if you have a big meeting, fellas put their heads down – they're afraid of saying things. What you want is some of them coming to you and saying, 'Look, this is the way things are.' So Brian, Paul, Ronan and Rory were voted in.

Sometimes players get names for being good captains because the team wins. Rory had been captain during a tough season for Ulster, but he stayed strong

through the whole lot of it, never made excuses – just said this is something we have to work through. I have huge time for somebody when I see them, in adversity, dealing with it that way.

LES KISS: Some players stood out for me straight away. The first was John Hayes. The man is a colossus. That's a great starting block, a number three like that. In Paul O'Connell I found a man who was driven, but who also had a mindset that was flexible enough to look at the game as a whole rather than just set-pieces – to look at different strategic approaches. He's a thinker. Then you had Brian, absolutely the best thirteen defender ever. The system that I put in place, he had to shift and shape how he has defended in the past. But he picked it up quickly and relished it. He's a guy who wants to push the boundaries.

DECLAN KIDNEY: I was talking to Brian in August. I said, 'You've been captain forty-eight times. You've looked after the team for years, but who has looked after you? Why don't you just forget about the captaincy for a while and just see can you enjoy it yourself? Do your own pre-season, don't worry about the other fellas.'

Because sometimes as a captain the others can lean on you too much. All I wanted to do was try and look after him. You take away some of the PR side and the sales and marketing side – because all that takes from the day. It allows him to rest up or to do a little bit more training, or just to concentrate on himself. If you've been captaining a side for that length of time and it's taken off you, you could be disappointed. But it could also free you up.

BRIAN O'DRISCOLL: For the first time in my life, I was a bit low in confidence. I spoke to a sports psychologist about it – sometimes you just need to hear someone saying nice things about you. I met him four or five times, for an hour or an hour and a half at a time. There's a lot said in that space of time, and I don't want to disrespect him but if you get three or four things out of that that you believe in, it's time well spent. He said a few things that really stuck with me. I had always, always backed my own ability, irrespective of what shape I was in or what the public perception was. I always felt that when it came to it I could produce. That's a confidence bordering on arrogance, but I don't apologize for it. So the beginning of the season was the first time I ever questioned myself.

'For the first time in my life, I was a bit low in confidence.'

ALAN GAFFNEY: There's no doubt there was a lack of confidence. He was a bit down in himself, Drico, following the previous season and the World Cup. He was marking his own card a bit harder than he should have. He had himself down that he wasn't playing that well – he was examining himself a bit too deeply. But I didn't agree with it. I was watching him from over in England and I didn't think he was all that far from playing well. It was just little things that weren't working

DECLAN KIDNEY: I got asked the question in August: who will be captain? I felt we had two or three fellas who could do it. So I said, 'We'll see in November.' Sometimes you don't make a decision until you have to.

CHAPTER 2
BUYING INTO THE JERSEY

BRIAN O'DRISCOLL: I've had my ups and downs with Declan through the years. But the Declan we see now is a very, very different Declan than in 2005. More knowledgeable, more understanding of his strengths, of what he can bring to a squad. He just has that unknown element about him that gets the best out of his teams. Back in 1998, we won the Under-19s World Cup under Declan and we were a long way from being the best team in the competition. We had to have done something right. I don't know what it is – it's very hard to put your finger on it.

ROB KEARNEY: Deccie's biggest strength is that he makes you feel good. You take to the pitch feeling confident – and that's 90 per cent of the battle.

ALAN GAFFNEY: He's got a very sharp brain. People don't give him credit for seeing through a lot of these problems and coming up with solutions, without making it a huge issue. Nothing's an issue with him. Or at least, the outward perception is that he remains very calm and very controlled in everything he does, in every decision he takes. He doesn't become perplexed. Maybe he does internally – maybe he goes back to his room and thumps the table.

DECLAN KIDNEY: When I was in my third year of coaching at Pres in Cork, we had thirty-six kids out training. I said to them, 'Right, when we get to Christmas we're going to reduce it to thirty.' That's what I did: I told six kids I couldn't train them. I will forever regret that – it's one that really gets to me. I should never, ever have done it. Who was I to tell them I wouldn't train them? They wanted to play just as much as professionals do today, if not more. That mistake was twenty-seven years ago, but it stays with me.

LEFT: As Declan Kidney took over, the captaincy of Brian O'Driscoll – who had suffered a dip in personal form and confidence – was in question

Back when I started coaching the school we used to train on the pitches up at Dennehy's Cross, in Wilton. Sergeant Waldron used to have the house at the side of the pitches. He would get a few Cyprus potatoes, put a bit of manure on them and sell them as his own. He was a retired sergeant and at that stage he was the curator for the church there. He'd come in and clean the dressing rooms as well. I vividly remember the day when he fell off a ladder fixing one of the crossbars and he couldn't help any more. After that I started sweeping up inside in the dressing room, because you had to have some bit of hygiene. Back then, you did what needed to be done, didn't matter what it was. There are all kinds of support roles in professional rugby now but when Munster played the Heineken Cup final in 2000 I was still bringing the balls to training in the boot of my car.

You learn things as you go along. You try to listen to people and you learn. You go in and you give it your best shot and when you get things wrong, it does eat you up. But if you let it, then you'll just get more wrong. You need to try and keep a bit of balance in your life. You know the highs and lows are huge and you have to swing with them from time to time. But if you can keep somewhere in the middle you can hold your sanity and stay there for a little bit longer.

When I started out, I was only a schools coach. After that it was a case of, 'He'll never manage it with club rugby.' Or, 'He'll never manage it with Munster.' Then it was: 'Can he can bring it from Munster to Ireland?' But no matter where I've been I've always seen my primary role as trying to help out the players and the people I work with, to allow them to do their job.

Sometimes we try to bracket people. I'm not an authority on backs play, or on forwards play – they're specialist roles. But I don't think I'm devoid of knowledge either. I've a fair idea as to how things work. You can't be a head coach if you don't understand all the different facets. How can I appreciate the work of specialist coaches if I don't understand it? But could I articulate it in that particular way? Maybe not. No one person can do everything, but if he is empowering people to do a job then I think that is a reasonable talent to have.

If there is somebody there with you who can do it – and you feel they can do it better than you – then you'd do the team more service by stepping aside. So, no problem. This is a big job and you need good people around you. When I worked with Brian O'Brien he said to me: 'You can only be as successful as the people around you want you to be.' I've been lucky, I've worked with a lot of good people.

ALAN GAFFNEY: He denigrates himself about his knowledge of rugby, but that is incorrect – he's very insightful. He definitely hasn't been given enough credit by a lot of people. It's something he may wish to hide, but in sitting down with Deccie and going through how we're going to do things, he has got a good knowledge of the game. We sit down and talk about what we're trying to do against Wales, against England – but he's the one who's got to make the final decision.

DECLAN KIDNEY: The bottom line with this job is that you're putting thirty-odd people in a room, where only fifteen of them can get selected, who all have their part to play in it and who are all human beings as well. Rugby coaches will want to do more, conditioning coaches will want to do less, medical staff will want no contact, operations will want you off the pitch because the media want to speak you. The job is co-ordinating all of that. I trust the people I work with, but at the end of the day I'm in charge of it. In the end, unless the players are looking forward to playing – and unless they have confidence in the way they are going to play – all the rest of it is rubbish. It doesn't count for anything.

> ❛When I started out, I was only a schools coach. After that it was a case of, 'He'll never manage it with club rugby.' Or, 'He'll never manage it with Munster.' Then it was: 'Can he can bring it from Munster to Ireland?'❜

As a player in top-class sport, you put yourself at the ledge. You leave yourself exposed to all sorts of things. And if the players who don't get selected aren't right, then that sours everything else. If you've got fellas dragging their arse around the dressing room, you don't have a team. So that's what I base it on – if I can get the players happy, we have a chance. And for them to be looking forward to the games, you have to have a bit of confidence in the way you're going to go about playing. Will it be the all-singing, all-dancing way that you'd love to play? No. You have to strike a balance.

You come in and you try and leave it in a better place. I've tried to do that in all the teams I've worked with.

BRIAN O'DRISCOLL: There was massive speculation about the captaincy. I wasn't getting myself caught up in it. All I could do was sit and wait and see. People were saying, 'Ah, he'll have less pressure if he's not captain. He'll concentrate on his own game.' But I had been captain for the previous five years. If people thought I was better during the first four years of my career than the years after I became captain, I would have to disagree. The big thing for me is that as captain you have to have the respect of your teammates and if that's wavering at all then I would have no interest. I asked certain people if I was still that person. For as long as I was – in their minds – then I was willing to do that job.

DECLAN KIDNEY: Brian went back playing. He was playing quite well. Just before Leinster played Wasps in the RDS, I said, 'Will you take on the captaincy again for the three games in November?'

BRIAN O'DRISCOLL: The thing about Declan – he plays it smart. He doesn't jump ahead of himself – there was another decision to be made for the Six Nations. I spoke to Paulie about it – I wanted to give it one last shot. It felt like there were capabilities for something special.

PAUL O'CONNELL: I said afterwards it was a non-issue for me – and it really was. I honestly didn't talk any less, or any more, than if I had been captain myself. There were times, I swear to God, when I'd say Brian felt he couldn't get a word in edgeways with me. Especially after we scored, because I always talked to the forwards after Munster scored. So I would just do the same, nearly forgetting I wasn't captain. It worked very well. I think – I hope – that it suited Brian.

DECLAN KIDNEY: The captaincy is a hugely important role but what I have learned over the years is that you have to have a few captains on the pitch if you are to be any way successful. When Munster won the Heineken Cup 2006 there was no huge public reason to change the captain, but Paul took over from Axel Foley. After a year he said, 'If I knew then what I know now...' As Munster captain Paul knew the importance of Axel's and Ronan's input. And the best compliment I can pay him is that, with Ireland, he was everything they were [for Munster]. And he will know how important that is. Everybody depends on everybody. That is the pure essence of the game. And I don't want that to be forgotten on my watch.

GORDON D'ARCY: I had a third operation on my arm in October. When I broke it [against Italy in February 2008] there were eight fractures and one of them didn't heal, so I had to have bone grafts. It was a difficult time. There were a lot of Chinese whispers about the injury. People were telling my brother and sister, 'Ah Jesus, your man D'Arcy is finished' – not knowing they were related to me. I had no real involvement with the Irish team until January, but Deccie stayed in touch with me.

I've known him since the Under-19s World Cup and I always felt I had a good rapport with the man. When I was younger he was somebody I was able to call for little bits and pieces of advice, when I didn't really know which way was up. He always gave me a straight answer – maybe not what I wanted to hear. Sometimes, he *did* tell you what you wanted to hear. That's the beauty of the man.

I can only speak for myself, but he's always got the best out of me. He picked his moments very well to call me and to stay in touch during the injury. He'd say, 'Listen, I don't want to be ringing you every week to see how you are. I know if there's something wrong somebody will tell me – and I'll call you then.' He kept a good bit of distance, but stayed in touch at the same time. When I was going in for the third operation he called me the day before. Again, that was good timing. It was nice to get a phone call to say, 'We're still thinking of you.'

MERVYN MURPHY: The trap that an international coaching team can fall into is not taking on board that these guys have come from a club environment where they are in meetings week in, week out for months on end. We get them at Tests and

we think, 'They're ours now and they should be fresh.' But they have come straight from that sort of stuff already. So you have big long meetings and you think, 'Why aren't they listening to us? Why are they nodding off?' They are coming off strenuous Heineken Cup matches where mentally there is an awful lot asked of them. It's important that the meetings are short and sharp and focused. They want you to explain why you're doing it and what it's supposed to achieve. And they're happy.

PAUL O'CONNELL: Deccie would never have been big into overanalysing teams or too many meetings. He was big on you worrying about yourself, getting yourself right. But we had a lot of meetings through the autumn, which would have been unDeccie-like. But I suppose he had coaches who wanted time and Deccie would be good at managing that. I'm sure if some people had their way there would have been a lot more meetings.

TOMMY BOWE: The thing I used to hate about Irish camp would be that you'd go in on a Sunday night and you'd be playing the following weekend, say England. From the Sunday night at eleven o'clock until kick-off on a Saturday it was 'England, England, England' and you couldn't get away from it. I enjoy going to training and being able to do my video work, but still being able to have my time to switch off. Under Declan we had more of that, which I enjoyed.

The team meetings were a lot different too. Whereas before they were very intense, this time they were long – two hours in the morning. I'm not the best morning person – sometimes I was just trying to stay awake. I'd roll out of a big,

❛ **People were telling my brother and sister, 'Ah Jesus, your man D'Arcy is finished' – not knowing they were related to me.** ❜

massive double bed, having stayed up half the night talking to my roommate. I'd be thinking, 'Jesus, I've only had a few hours' sleep.' Quickly get down to breakfast, try to scoop some eggs, fruit and everything into me and get down into the meeting, still trying to pull my eyes apart. We'd have a backs meeting, forty-five minutes long, then we'd have a five-minute break and go into the big team meeting room. We're watching the same stuff again, but talking about it as a full team. We're allowed to express our opinion.

As a team we collectively came to realize that it wasn't all about what the coach wanted us to do. If we disagreed with what he was saying, we were allowed to stick our hands up and question it. That was something I hadn't felt up to then. Before, I would have been afraid even to think about opening my mouth. You were just sitting there and concentrating more on trying to stay awake, rather than thinking, 'Maybe I have something that can improve it.'

GERT SMAL: It was early days. We'd hadn't worked with the players much and we felt the autumn series was going to teach us a fair amount, about their physical and mental make-up. As a coaching staff we had got to know each other a little better. We'd started challenging each other more, but we'd had very little time with the players. There was an awful lot of work ahead of us.

JERRY FLANNERY: We were trying to rebuild, to get our basic basics right. Of the three November internationals, the Canadian game at Thomond Park wasn't so much of a test for us. We couldn't get a true feel for where we were as a side, but a win is a win, you know. You have to start getting wins to get confidence back – morale was very low for the previous eighteen months.

We run two teams in training and if you're on the same team as Paul O'Connell and Ronan O'Gara and Brian O'Driscoll, then it's looking good. I was in the other team. Then Declan announced it – and I was in. I thought, 'Jesus, this is brilliant!' Because it came out of nowhere. We won the match [55–0] and I thought I played well.

The following Monday, the day before the team to play the All Blacks was picked, I was driving out of the Castletroy Park Hotel, on my way into the bar to meet my dad. The phone rang. Declan Kidney.

You know what's coming. You know that when you sit down with him, nothing is going to change his mind. You're going in there thinking, 'What can I get out of this that's going to make it a more positive situation for me?' You ask whatever hard questions you can come up with that will help you deal with it – and get back in the team.

On the evening before every Ireland international match players make their way to the room of Paddy 'Rala' O'Reilly, who is listed in match programmes as the squad's 'baggage master'. That's bagman for short, but the service he provides defies a job title. Among other things, he's responsible for vast quantities of official gear for on and off the pitch, but his most important function has nothing to do with jerseys, shorts and socks.

PADDY 'RALA' O'REILLY: I've been the Ireland bagman for fifteen seasons now. It's almost like being a butler. Remember *Upstairs Downstairs* from years ago? I'd be

like Hudson. The master would ring, looking for toast or something. I'm only using that as an example. With me it would be a lace or a stud. It's like trying to be in the background, but trying to keep an eye on them – and help them. That's what you're there for. Maybe they come to my room because they want to talk to someone. I wouldn't know really, I'm just a lay person.

DENIS LEAMY: He's really there for the players. He plays the fool, but he's no fool. If he wasn't good at his job he wouldn't last, but he's able to incorporate both that and the other side of it – and he adds something extra. Players love him. Anything we need, it's never a problem. It's a good room to call to, listening to him going on and on about his experiences in Inishbofin and getting a few jellies off him.

DONNCHA O'CALLAGHAN: We call him The Slug – because he moves as slow as a snail but he wouldn't even carry a house. He carries nothing. He's the world's best delegator, Rala. You talk to any hotel porter and I'd say they hate him. He just stands there with a fag hanging out of his mouth, pointing the direction he wants stuff to go in. But the man forgets nothing, he has everything covered.

‘Shane Horgan used to say it, and it's so true: ‘A happy Rala is a happy camp.’

Shane Horgan used to say it, and it's so true: ‘A happy Rala is a happy camp.’ If Rala isn't happy, if his room isn't right or something, everything should be done to change it. Because when people go to Rala and he's in great form, we all feed off it. If Rala is down, our heads are dropping as well.

We often say, ‘Go on, pick Rala's all-time Ireland XV. Ah go on, Rala – who would you have in the front row?’ Because you would give *anything* to be on Rala's XV. It wouldn't come down to rugby – it would come down to your character as a person. Me and Marcus are constantly trying to get it out of him; probably because he was so tight with other guys in our positions we know we're nowhere near it.

RORY BEST: On that night before we played the All Blacks, there was a bit of a feeling in the camp. We thought we had the beating of them. We thought, ‘Definitely – we have them here.’ It would have been a great start for the new coaching staff to come in and beat New Zealand.

DECLAN KIDNEY: The players really wanted to win and they took on a load of information. But we forgot that the opposition were going to turn up as well. They were just more physical than us. We were a long way from being the worst against them in the autumn but you might say that's clutching at straws.

LES KISS: For the November series we had the situation where could have dropped down a place to ninth in the world rankings and been third seeds for the next World Cup. That was pressure and we just had to deliver eighth position – which meant we had to beat Argentina.

Three days after Ireland's 22–3 defeat to New Zealand at Croke Park, Munster took on the All Blacks at Thomond Park. Thirty years had passed since their

predecessors in the red jersey shocked the rugby world by beating Graham Mourie's otherwise undefeated tourists 12–0. Now the Munster heroes from 1978 sat together at the front of the East Stand in the magnificent new stadium as a Munster team minus a string of big names dug a monumental performance out of themselves, perhaps driven by the fear of humiliation. Magnificently captained by Mick O'Driscoll, they came within four minutes of victory. Among the spectators was Ronan O'Gara and like everyone else in the ground he was awed by a ferocious, unyielding Munster effort.

At a press conference two days later, back in Dublin, he contrasted the respective performances of Ireland and Munster and his conclusion could scarcely have been more pointed. 'We need to play as a team and for each other,' he said about Ireland. 'We need to start buying into the Irish jersey a little more.'

DECLAN KIDNEY: I was at the match at Thomond Park too and it was hugely emotional. When someone says something, it can be interpreted in different ways by different people, depending on the way they say it – the tone of voice. Then you write it down and there can be other perceptions. The particular sentence he came out with, I knew it was open to interpretation, depending on what different people wanted to interpret out of it.

It was a frustration within him. That's Ronan. We've known each other a long time. Do we always go the exact same road? No. But somebody once said: if everybody's thinking the same, then nobody's thinking. Team leaders have a different view of what they need to bring and without his input we wouldn't be where we are now. But I wouldn't speak on Ronan's behalf. He'll give you his own motivations for saying what he said.

RONAN O'GARA: I was invited into that press conference with Deccie and Brian. Why did I say it? Because there was an Irish jersey there and from my point of view the value of it wasn't being truly appreciated. It's harder to win at international level than at provincial level. I felt that the effort required to win wasn't where it needed to be. My comments were in relation to the Munster versus All Blacks game. I have a great relationship with the Munster forwards on the Irish team, so you can be sure that I was questioning a lot of the Munster players – as well as myself.

I had said it to the players the day previously, in a huddle. There was no immediate reaction. I didn't go to town on my point – I just said it. I've made points before to the group where people have been taken aback or slightly stunned – but there was no reaction to this. The reaction of the press is obviously something you can't control and the truth is that I had no idea of the impact it would have. I'm beginning to realize that if you are playing well, your words carry a bit of weight. But then again if you start thinking like that you fall in love with yourself – and that's a trait I don't like in anybody.

There was a small bit of frustration there as well – and that was as a result of not winning things with Ireland. You can go away and win three games in the Six Nations, beat Australia now and then, beat South Africa, fail to New Zealand – and still stay at the same level. And the clock was ticking, not just for me but for the group. So that's why it was said. Did I feel better after I said it? No. Did it mean anything? No, not really. I say plenty of things but they don't become public knowledge and I don't want them to. The most important thing to me was the team. If the team goes well, I go well. And that's how we win things.

Kidney moved quickly to downplay O'Gara's comments once they made headlines the following day. The senior players, he said carefully, could sometimes be too self-critical for their own good. And apart from that, Rog was Rog. Searing honesty was part of the package. Meanwhile, the players had to face down an Argentina side who were now ranked fourth in the world and who had contributed handsomely to the misery of Ireland's World Cup.

JERRY FLANNERY: I got twenty minutes against the All Blacks and then I got back in for Argentina. Paulie pulled us and said, 'Look, all we have to do is win this game. That's all.'

DECLAN KIDNEY: It was a shocker of a match. We went the opposite road to the performance against New Zealand. We went out there to make sure that we didn't get ourselves beaten up. We did what we had to do. We won.

> ‘ **There was an Irish jersey there and from my point of view the value of it wasn't being truly appreciated.** ’

LES KISS: There was a turnover in that Argentina game where Paul went into a ruck and won the ball. Straight away all the players came together, slapping each other on the back. There was a lot riding on that game and it was very striking, seeing that. It didn't result in a score and we weren't at the stage where the game was in the balance. I saw the roar of emotion that came from Paul. It was about a moment of dominance.

MARK TAINTON: We won by a spread, more than one score [17–3]. And we hadn't done that before against them. So I tried to tell the rest of the coaching team, 'This is going to bring confidence. You don't understand what that scoreline will bring to the players.'

JERRY FLANNERY: People panned us after it, but I was just saying, 'Look, we've been losing games for so long. The only thing that matters is results.' Individual performance is important for a player, because you're not going to keep playing if you don't deliver. But if you keep winning, people can't be complaining.

The most damning criticism came from the RTÉ rugby panel. They were in no doubt: the match had been an abomination, and despite the recruitment of a high-powered new coaching team there was zero evidence that Ireland were improving. The backline had no shape, the forwards weren't running at people. 'One of the worst games you've ever seen Ireland play?' suggested Tom McGurk to Brent Pope. Correction, said Pope, it was one of the worst games he had ever seen, full stop.

   'The real worry about this,' said George Hook, 'is just how bad Ireland were. This match shows that we are now susceptible to Scotland, Wales, England and France – and maybe even Italy.'

LEFT: A typical moment in a brutal match: Argentina's Juan Manuel Leguizamón cuffs Brian O'Driscoll, who is already sporting a shiner

The senior Ireland players who had been involved in dogfights with Argentina down the years had a different take on it. For them, a 14-point victory against the team ranked fourth in the world – no matter the manner in which it had been achieved – was evidence of an upturn.

PAUL O'CONNELL: We produced a very good win. There are a few guys in the team whose opinion I'd trust more than anyone else's – and we were very happy, despite what the media may have said. The media told us not to be happy with it.

KARL RICHARDSON, MEDIA MANAGER: There was a huge amount of criticism on TV and in the press after the Argentina game. Some players pay attention to it, some don't. But whether they read the press or not, it filters in from family and friends. Declan said it to the media after the Argentina game. 'Don't underestimate the effect that you guys have on the team.'

MARCUS HORAN: Every player that I've played with has been affected by the press at some stage in their career. We're all human and you have to deal with it – but it is hard to deal with. It's another factor in trying to prepare for a game – trying to block out what is being said about you.

BRIAN O'DRISCOLL: Something you have to understand as captain is that your fellow players read what you're saying, so you have to say certain things that your team-mates are going to believe. Whether you want to say them or not. No matter what emotions you're feeling yourself, you have to present a persona of confidence and calm. Because people still read papers.

TOMMY BOWE: When I was a kid my dad used to take me to Lansdowne Road and after I'd seen the match I used to love reading the player ratings in the papers. Sometimes I'd agree with what they were saying, sometimes I wouldn't. One paper would say one thing, another would say a different thing.

I got my first cap when I was twenty. It was a great day for me. I scored a try and I was delighted. I thought it was all going to be great, but even then there were questions. Has he got enough pace? Is he good enough for this level? It does you no good reading these things. There was no definite point where I said, 'That's the end of it, no more of that', but over time I decided to try and stay away from it.

Sometimes, though, it was hard to avoid it. You'd get text messages from friends. A few years back I got dropped after playing against France. I was trying to forget about the match, trying to keep to myself, to keep my spirits up a bit ...

Ah, it wasn't that bad. Just forget about it. It wasn't THAT bad.

Then I got a text.

Jesus I can't believe it! The Tribune gave you zero out of ten!!!

I think that's a world record. I've never seen anybody get a zero out of ten before. They didn't do zero out of ten when I was a boy going to Lansdowne Road.

MARCUS HORAN: A young guy trying to make his way in the game – to have that done to him was a disgrace. But it will never change. I've been through it all, the highs and lows. The slap in the back you get from some people isn't too far away from a kick in the hole. We were always taught that.

TWO

59

CHAPTER

‘ **There's so much more to the game than meets the eye on the television. There's a lot more behind the scenes.** ’

> *The slap in the back you get from some people isn't too far away from a kick in the hole. We were always taught that.*

Rugby has hit phenomenal heights in the last ten years. It's hitting a demographic now that never saw it before – and they need their opinions. There's nowhere better to get that than in the newspapers – people do regurgitate a lot of that stuff. Then there's the TV analysts.

BRIAN O'DRISCOLL: I have a reasonable amount of respect for Brent Pope because I think he calls it as he sees it. He doesn't feel the need to overindulge himself in disseminating his views. Conor O'Shea – I've played with Conor, I think he has a good understanding of the game. I think Brent has a good understanding of the game. George Hook, to a degree, knows what's going on – but I don't necessarily feel what he thinks in his head is what he says out of his mouth. They can be two very different things.

JERRY FLANNERY: Whether it's accurate of not, it doesn't affect me. The people who matter are the coaches and the players. I never judge myself off what papers say. It's just the personal stuff that I think is rubbish. Once it has to do with rugby, I don't care.

ROB KEARNEY: There's so much more to the game than meets the eye on the television. There's a lot more behind the scenes.

RONAN O'GARA: People have a fair idea of what's going on. They can sense moods and form in the camp and they have an idea of who's playing well. Because the media say something about a player's performance doesn't necessarily mean it's true. But a lot of the time the media do get it right in terms of who's hot and who's cold. Down in Munster we were always told that you'll never beat

the media, and they'll always be there. I'd have private feelings on a good few of the rugby journalists over the years. I do read the stuff. I'd be pretty up to date on it. There were days when it annoyed the hell out of me, others when it was water off a duck's back.

KARL RICHARDSON: Before the World Cup there was a lot of confidence in the squad. The question was asked, 'Can you win it?' A lot of people said, 'Yes – why not?' Because there had been performances to back that up. But when you have lofty aspirations and you make them public, if you don't reach those targets then everything is a failure.

It does upset me sometimes. Maybe I shouldn't say that, but yes. I have to put these guys in front of the media and sometimes they get blasted. Sometimes they might not want to do interviews but I have to say, 'Guys, you've got to.' And then they'll say, 'I had to do media and they're killing us in the press.'

I'm up at the crack of dawn to read the papers, online first and then down to the shop. I've an insatiable curiosity to find out what they're saying. We don't expect propaganda – fans with typewriters – but they can have a big influence on what supporters think.

ROB KEARNEY: You never like to be critical of fans because they are the people who go and watch you – they're the critics at the end of the day.

JERRY FLANNERY: The basic principles of the game are the same from schools rugby up to internationals, but when you move up the levels there are tiny things that make a huge difference.

LUKE FITZGERALD: The margins are so small, they're minuscule. The guys on the other side are putting in the hours trying to break you down as well. A huge amount of credit has to be given to the backroom staff. I couldn't really see a coaching staff working any harder. There's a serious amount of hours put into figuring things out.

MERVYN MURPHY: There has been a phenomenal change, unbelievable. I've been involved eight years and it has only really come that way in the last four. I think

it's because space is at such a premium now, you've got to go into a scrum or a lineout knowing exactly what you are going to be doing and it's got to be precise if it's going to work. It is an exact science. You've got to have clarity before you walk onto the Test field. All these micro details – if they are all right, then everything becomes much more clear. It's like putting a jigsaw together. If all the pieces are in the right place, you get a clear picture. But if there are a couple of pieces missing, you can't see it properly.

You need to be intelligent at this level and the intelligent guys are the guys that do well – players who can marry intelligence with aggression. Paul O'Connell is a brilliant example of that. He's a master at analysis. It's unbelievable the hours he puts in with Gert Smal, trying to crack codes, looking for cues. The way you crack somebody's code is to work and work and work on it. He looks at things like the hooker who might have a certain way of throwing the ball, a certain twitch just before his delivery. There might be a nod from how a jumper gives notice that he's ready, a clap of the hands, a front movement, a back movement. Gert spends an incredible amount of time in the analysis room. Hours can go by and the guy is still sitting there. I've never seen anything like it.

Players are now under so much peer pressure to be smart because if you don't get it right – if you miss a lineout movement or a lineout call, or get the menu mixed up – the other players will go through you. If there's a backline move and you're not in the right position, you should be picked out at the next meeting and asked, 'Why weren't you there? How did you miss that?' So you need to be concentrating 100 per cent on every one of these micro details.

JOHN HAYES: When Merv started, he had a VCR machine. A DHL van would pull up outside the house with a package. Inside would be a video cassette, you'd put it into your television and watch what you did in the match. It was a novelty at that stage.

MERVYN MURPHY: These days you could be in the office from 9 a.m. to midnight every day analysing matches, breaking them down. We have an analysis room with eight Apple Macs. We're trying to find holes, and come up with plays that will get into those holes. We're analysing the referee, everything. We spend a lot of time on phonetics. A player is trying to communicate a play with a mouthguard and a load of saliva in his mouth, so you have a word that is easy for him to say, and doesn't sound like another word. Some letters are very distinct – S, T, K, P – and that's what you need. Even if it comes out a bit muffled, they've heard the sound of it. Sometimes it'll be something the opposition think they know, because they think it'll be what it sounds like – but it's actually the complete opposite. There are all sorts of moves you can go into to play with the opposition's heads. I could be here all night talking about that.

They all understand the value of it. Eight years ago, I had one Apple Mac and I got the odd player looking at it. Now, every single one of them study analysis. They feel if they didn't do it, they'd be letting down the team. The players who work hardest at this are the players who end up performing better than the others. I can say that for a fact. Some guys might have had the attitude, 'I don't need to study analysis, I rely on my own ability to read a situation.' You used to have a lot of that. It's all changed now. They're all in there, studying it. They feel they dare not let their teammates down.

EOIN TOOLAN, ASSISTANT PERFORMANCE ANALYST: Paul O'Connell and Donncha O'Callaghan are hugely competitive and when the individual performance stats come out on a Tuesday or Wednesday – from the amount of rucks they hit to the amount of tackles they made – those two guys are the first in to see who beat who. Paul is obviously a huge player for us but Donncha's stats are phenomenal as well – he does a lot of the graft and the unseen work. He puts his body on the line for the team. He's the heartbeat of the team, I think. Such a character.

GERT SMAL: It's always been my philosophy – and I think Declan's too – that the quicker you can make your players independent of you the better, so that they can make independent decisions. Because when the pressure is on, that's what they are going to have to do. Sometimes you want to give a message to the players and you can't get it there quickly enough. So they have to think on their feet, read situations, have a feel for the physical state of the team at a certain stage of the game and make decisions accordingly. The players are the best to get that feel. That's the way I was brought up in my playing career. As a player, you don't want to be told all the time what to do, especially when you have experienced players. It's a different thing when you don't – then you may be a little bit more structured. But experienced players, they've been there already.

RONAN O'GARA: The game has changed. Now it's counter-attack, it's phase play. A good thing about playing out-half is that essentially it falls back on me. If things go well, I'm praised. If things don't go well, who's the first to cop it? Me. I've been around long enough to realize that. You have to change it at times and do what you think is right. But that's the beauty of playing 10. Yes, it is detailed. But then, when it's played well, it's so simple.

LES KISS: At the end of November, we understood where things sat. As coaches we'd found out a lot about ourselves in terms of the way we all operated. But the bottom line is: between us we've got a lot of knowledge, but it's not about what *we* know. If the players can't do it on the footy field it means nothing. We had to build something that suited the strengths of the players and that process was still happening. It mightn't have looked it to some people, but we were starting to get somewhere and the confidence the players got from beating Argentina was important.

‘ **Some guys might have had the attitude, 'I don't need to study analysis, I rely on my own ability to read a situation.' You used to have a lot of that. It's all changed now.** ’

Slowly, their belief levels were starting to come back. Now I don't think they had been totally destroyed or anything. You can't win a Heineken Cup and a Magners League the year before if your confidence is that low. There had been a wonderful period and maybe it didn't finish well for Eddie O'Sullivan, but he did a fantastic job. But I found in a collective sense, their confidence was lacking – certainly. Having said that, I knew it was bubbling underneath.

GERT SMALL: In the early stages, the players didn't share as much as they could have. They wanted new things, they didn't want to do the same things. But we thought at the time that they could have participated a little bit more, given the experience that they had. I think they were waiting for the coaching staff to come up with new ideas, but your experience as a player is worth nothing if you can't share.

‘ **We still needed to clear some lines, give them clarity of purpose and direction.** ’

RONAN O'GARA: When you have fellas thinking about the game, offering input, then you've a really good team – because everyone is challenging each other and thinking about it. We can argue, we can discuss it, but you can be sure that at the end of the day we can find the right solution. But if there's only one or two fellas thinking about the game, well then you've a team of robots.

LES KISS: What the November series said to me about the players was this. Intent? Wonderful. Attitude? Absolutely brilliant – they wanted to go somewhere new. Capacity? It had to be pulled into something that had meaning, something that was purposeful. We still needed to clear some lines, give them clarity of purpose and direction. And that's what the camp at Enfield turned out to be about.

CHAPTER 3
A PLAN COMES TOGETHER

' Say what you think, guys. '

For Kidney and his coaches, facing into their first Six Nations together, time with the players was precious. On Monday, 12 December, tired and battle-weary after successive Heineken Cup weekends, they came together for a short international camp. The usual location for Ireland's pre-Christmas training was one where the sun shines in winter: Portugal or Lanzarote. Kidney and McNaughton opted for the Marriott Johnstown House Hotel in Enfield, Co. Meath. Far from happy with the autumn performances and concerned by the players' continuing lack of confidence, they believed there was more need for talking than training.

At the time, the camp merited barely a mention. Three months later, in the afterglow of Grand Slam glory, Enfield became news. An honest exchange of views between Munster and Leinster players about passion – about the red jersey and the green – found its way, belatedly, into the papers. In the fairy-tale version, this became the theme that dominated the Enfield camp and the defining reason for Ireland's triumphant turnaround. In reality, it lasted thirty-five minutes over the course of a three-day get-together.

Everything had been up for discussion – from the smallest logistical issues to bigger decisions such as where the squad trained. All on the table.

PAUL McNAUGHTON: We felt it would be better to keep it at home, keep it sharp – and keep them off their feet and off the training paddock for most of it. There was general dissatisfaction among the coaches about the way we had played in November. There were guys not playing well, a lot of poor execution. We had achieved the world ranking we needed, but it wasn't pretty and we weren't going

THREE
69
CHAPTER

LEFT: Rob Kearney and Brian O'Driscoll

❝ The difference between winning a Grand Slam and coming third or fourth is the stuff you do off the pitch. ❞

to do well in the Six Nations if we continued like that. We thought we needed to talk about it, so that we wouldn't be navel-gazing in January. It was too late to navel-gaze then.

RORY BEST: The senior players were asked to be in Enfield three or four hours ahead of the rest of the squad for a meeting with Declan and Paul McNaughton. It was tough enough at the time, everyone was tired off the back of two European Cup games and it was coming up to Christmas. But a lot came out of that meeting in terms of what was going to happen over the next couple of days and how we were going to play in the Six Nations.

As a rugby player you can sometimes think that your role is just to go out and play a bit of ball on a pitch. But the higher up you go, the lines become finer. The difference between winning a Grand Slam and coming third or fourth is the stuff you do off the pitch. Often, it's a failsafe for when something goes wrong. How do you react? You have to react quickly and having it all down in our notebooks and in our laptops helps to ensure there are no grey areas.

We wanted to take it back to the day when Irish camp was a great place to be, when you looked forward to it. Since the World Cup, that hadn't been the case. Maybe we felt we still had the tag of failures. But it wasn't a great place to turn up to and even though we'd got new coaches, there was still a bit of it hanging around in the autumn.

PAUL MCNAUGHTON: When Declan and I sat down with the four senior players there was a good frank discussion, and the most important thing was that it was decided we would stick at it and get all of these issues out of the way, rather than just go back on the training field and go through the motions for the next two days.

DECLAN KIDNEY: I didn't take the job to walk on eggshells, or to just stay in the job. I took it to do the best I could. And I thought we were going nowhere, so we needed to find out what the story was. I was with fellas I'd worked with before, but they didn't have any confidence. They're good players, so what's the problem? Let's sit down and talk about it. And if you don't want to say what the problem is, then fine. Get on with it yourself. Because I have no interest in being around.

They'd had six good years and won three Triple Crowns. They weren't complimenting themselves enough about that achievement. I have a lot of time for us in Ireland, I think we're a right intelligent nation. One reason it's a good place to live is because we don't go overboard. We'll always tell you the thing that's wrong, but you need to tell yourself what's going right as well. I think the thing is to enjoy ourselves – and they weren't enjoying it as much as they could. So what's the problem?

PAUL MCNAUGHTON: You have an international team who have been around for five or six years with the same coaching set-up. They've done well – but they haven't

satisfied their ambitions. They've come off a bad World Cup. You could argue some of them would go back to the comfort of their own clubs – because that was a more successful place to be. And then the idea that a totally new coaching team would come along and have five days in August, then pitch up in November and beat the hell out of everybody, was something out of fantasy land. What actually happened was: we had our week in August, we spluttered around in the dark in November, then we came together in December, like a corporation on an off-site, looking for some answers.

DECLAN KIDNEY: How do you provide the facility to let it come out? If there were boils there and we were going to lance them, were we going to get all the pus out? We split them into different groups: front five, middle five, back five. We had facilitators in each group, senior players. The coaches had their own group.

GERT SMAL: It's a thing that a team has to go through, at some stage. We did it at the right time. We had the same thing with the Boks. The Bulls and the Sharks,

> **We had our week in August, we spluttered around in the dark in November, then we came together in December, like a corporation on an off-site, looking for some answers.**

those two teams grew together. You could see them playing for each other. And unless you have that in a national set-up, you won't be successful. Enfield brought us much closer together, as coaching staff and as players. From then onwards there was more purpose and more clarity about the way we wanted to play.

We thought – I thought – that in the autumn series things would happen much quicker because we had the experience as coaches and as players. It didn't work that way. So when we got together in Enfield, a lot of different aspects and dynamics were discussed. It's the same kind of thing that any company does when they are trying to bring employees together. We didn't have a professional facilitator – you normally get someone who's not attached to the organization. Declan did it. One of his strengths is to listen to a lot of points of view and then pull it all together at the end.

MERVYN MURPHY: Sometimes I get a bit cringey at big meetings where things are written up on boards. It can feel like David Brent in *The Office*. I'd been there before and I was thinking, 'Is this the same old stuff again?' But it was a lot more cutting edge.

LES KISS: We didn't know where it was going to go, but we had to explore some things and ask the hard questions. And this is the vital thing: if you tell them, 'Say what you think, guys. Let's open it up and see where it goes', then you've got to cop it, you've got to listen and you've got to find out where you stand in it. There had to be a place where there was trust and where people could talk freely. You might be wrong, but it's not about right and wrong, it's about finding out what people are thinking.

LEFT: Les Kiss

You've got to be careful too, because you get a lot of things, a huge list of stuff. The true art of it is pulling out the real things. People were saying things like, 'We've got to improve our passing left to right.' But that wasn't the issue then. The issues were – what does this mean to us and how do we take it forward? I firmly believe that if you don't have what the players got going – and what Declan drove – then it doesn't matter what else you've got. It can't work.

RORY BEST: Paul went with the back-rows and scrum-halves so I was in charge of the front-fives. I opened up the floor and took notes. 'If there's anything on your chest, throw it out.' Malcolm O'Kelly and Jerry had a lot to say, Marcus too. Everything from training to stuff we do on our days off. No real order, no rhythm or reason to it, just a case of getting it all out and handing over the sheets to Declan.

PAUL O'CONNELL: We were given headings to discuss but they were really vague – classic Deccie. He'd deliberately leave it vague and hope someone uncovers a gem. We were laughing and joking at the start, we couldn't figure out what to do. Deccie came over to us.

DECLAN KIDNEY: They were saying, 'What are we to talk about? You haven't told us anything.' I said, 'That's exactly it. You talk about what's on your mind.'

STEPHEN FERRIS: We put ideas down about everything – and that was what he wanted in the end. The biggest thing was our game plan, trying to get something simplified, something everyone was going to buy into. After an hour, Declan came over.
    'Are yez ready, lads?'
    'No, no. Give us another five minutes.'
    Another half an hour goes by.
    'Ready now, lads?'
    'No, no. Come back to us.'

DECLAN KIDNEY: I couldn't get them to finish because there was a load of stuff coming out. After that the idea was to get the facilitators to stand up and go through the issues.

Rob Kearney, twenty-two years old and an international player since only the summer of 2007, was in the back-five group facilitated by Ronan O'Gara, who by then had represented his country eighty-seven times. As O'Gara attempted to tease out the issues, Kearney pointed to the elephant in Ireland's team room. In doing so, he articulated something that had hung in the air for years, without ever being openly said. He told the rest of his group that whenever he watched Munster from his armchair at home, it seemed to him that there was a spirit about them, a special bond that sometimes made the difference between defeat and victory. The insinuation was obvious, but Kearney spelled it out anyway: if the same spirit could be instilled in the Ireland jersey they would all be going places, together.

O'Gara noted the comment. Three weeks previously, he had made the same point himself, more or less, when he spoke about the Munster players 'buying into the Irish jersey a little more'. But this had a sharper edge, because of where it was coming from. Still, O'Gara did not take offence. It was, he thought, a fair question for a Leinster player to be asking. When they broke for a coffee, he let Marcus Horan know what had been raised. The comment had not been intended as a dig, he stressed – in fact, he had detected a certain envy in Kearney. No matter: it did not sit well with the Munster loosehead.

Minutes later, in front of the entire squad, O'Gara was asked by Kidney to share the points raised by his discussion group. The significance of Kearney's contribution was not lost on him and he disclosed the sentiment, but did not reveal the source.

'It's good to have that out on the table,' said Kidney. Horan spoke next. He was offended, he said. Anyone who thought he gave anything less than his all for Ireland didn't know him. For Munster, he gave everything; for his country, he offered nothing less. Ireland for him was the ultimate: always had been, always would.

Now Kearney stood up and identified himself as the player who had made the comment. He began to defend it, to explain it. At first, as he heard the words coming out of his mouth, he was thinking, 'Maybe I should just stop now and run out the door.' He felt vulnerable because of his inexperience. Eleven caps to his name and there he was, talking the talk to players with eighty or ninety. He stood his ground and walked the walk. He wasn't questioning the commitment of the

'Listen, I think you've solved a massive problem for this squad. It's been festering for years and someone needed to say it.'

Munster players when they put on a green jersey – he just wanted to see the Ireland team come together in the same way.

LES KISS: When change happens, there are going to be challenges to overcome. You have to feel ... not so much safe, but you have to trust something. And the first thing he trusted was himself. He let himself feel it and he put it there. The environment allowed it to happen, but it takes courage. Courage from a young man to stand up and say that. It was about redefining the green and what it meant to them. You sat there and you saw the other groups leaning forward to make sure they heard everything.

RORY BEST: It seemed a bit strange to me but I remember thinking, 'Fair play, that's clearly what Rob was feeling and it's good that he's thrown it out there.' But it would never have even crossed my mind to question the passion the Munster forwards have playing for Ireland.

JOHN HAYES: Nobody ever lost the passion to play for Ireland. When we played England at Croke Park in 2007, nobody questioned us then. Playing for Ireland is unbelievable. I've played ninety-something times for my country and I still get as nervous as I did at the start of my career. I don't know why we didn't perform at the World Cup, but it wasn't down to passion. No one turned off the passion switch.

PAUL O'CONNELL: If the Munster forwards appeared not to play with passion with Ireland for the last few years, it was because we didn't really play the game through the forwards. So because we started taking teams on up front a little bit in the Six Nations, maybe the Munster players appeared to be playing better. We weren't whipping it out to the backs every time, running across, recovering the ball in

a ruck and then whipping it out to the backs again. If we were, it would still appear the same.

MARCUS HORAN: We went out training that day and we were strolling back – myself and Donncha and Rob. Donncha turned to Rob and said, 'Look, man, great balls today.' And I said, 'Listen, I think you've solved a massive problem for this squad. It's been festering for years and someone needed to say it.'

It really struck a chord with me. It was something you would have expected from an older guy. But then again, an older guy probably wouldn't have said it because he's lived with it for so long. When you have young guys like that in the team, you know you can get on with your own job without worrying about them. But it wasn't like guys were hugging each other in tears. It was just said, done, over with.

ROB KEARNEY: It was taken positively and you do appreciate that. Fair play to the Munster lads – not one person had anything negative to say. It takes character to take that on board and channel it positively.

BRIAN O'DRISCOLL: The Enfield factor was big. There were things that needed to be put right after the November series. We weren't fully understanding of where we needed to be and Enfield sorted a lot of that out. The game plan was way more important than the other things that were said, but it was great that there was really good honesty.

I knew Kearns was a bit worried about it coming out [in the press]. I rang him and said, 'Listen, understand that there is no negativity to be had about this. People are going to respect you as a young guy coming out and saying that.' Because you hear about the Saipan thing and the way Roy Keane was fobbed off, about all the young guys who stayed quiet. People like Ian Harte went to his room afterwards, but for a guy to front up in front of everyone, that takes balls. Whether they are in agreement or not is neither here nor there. It's about a guy willing to put his neck on the line and say what he's really thinking.

TOMMY BOWE: I didn't get released by the Ospreys [for the Enfield meeting] – it was outside the IRB ruling of dates you had to be released for. I was on the phone to the guys and it sounded incredibly serious. Maybe we covered our eyes a little bit to the

real issues we had in the autumn, but at the time I didn't think there was anything wrong and I was surprised there was this kind of crisis meeting being held. You're locked in and the key has been thrown away – so get your woes and problems out. That's the way it came across to me. One part of me was thinking, 'I've missed something really important here.' But another part of me was almost thankful: 'Maybe I'm lucky. Jesus, things aren't *that* bad.'

LES KISS: There was no malice. It was just, 'This is reality.' Now, Jesus, that starts to open up a few opportunities, doesn't it? Once people communicate in that way, you've got an opportunity to develop something, critical points that transcend rugby. So any type of technical or tactical platform you want to develop further comes off the back of that.

It wasn't going to guarantee anything. There was some work to be done. But the French game was the one where we could put it on the table. We'd found a bit of our mojo, things were starting to align.

DECLAN KIDNEY: It wasn't just about the Munster thing – far from it. There was an awful lot more to Enfield than that, a lot of other things said and nobody's nervous system was left untouched. But if they didn't want it to work, they wouldn't have said half of what they did.

PAUL O'CONNELL: The meetings at Enfield gave us belief that we as a pack were running the ship a lot more than we had. That's the beauty of teams and how they are successful. The more guys you have with opinions and the more guys you have who want to be involved in how the game is played – even if you have people who are disagreeing – you can come to a happy medium and go forward. My opinion is that when the pack is performing, you can play football after that. Really successful teams come when you have maybe five guys who can be equally driven, but might have fairly different views – and yet they can pull together. You need guys who can see the value in other people's views. If you don't agree, you don't just walk out the door.

DECLAN KIDNEY: There's no reason to say we can't take on teams up front. But there's no way you are going to take on any team up front for eighty minutes.

> **The meetings at Enfield gave us belief that we as a pack were running the ship a lot more than we had.**

Paul said years ago that rugby is the decathlon of team sports and that's a great way of describing it. How much time do you spend on which things? How much emphasis do you put on the different aspects in your game plan? As the head coach, that's my call.

LUKE FITZGERALD: There was a feeling, especially among the backs, that we needed to back ourselves a bit more in terms of going at teams and running the ball.

PAUL MCNAUGHTON: It's all very well saying, 'Let's run the ball all over the place.' But did we have the team to do that? And was it the right thing to do to win Test matches? We knew we had to play better football than we had in November, but we also had to be realistic. There were contradictions in different people's views. It was a matter of taking all of that on board and coming up with a game plan that had the pack taking on other packs, but not in our own bloody twenty-two. You spend half an hour beating the hell out of each other, but where are you? Still in your own twenty-two. There were three or four different views and it was Kidney's skill to take the visions of different players – and the inconsistencies – and come up with something they all bought into.

DECLAN KIDNEY: One of the things that came out was about getting field position. At first they misunderstood what I meant. They said, 'That means you want us to kick everything in our own half.' I said, 'I don't – not at all. I just don't want to be making it easy for the opposition. Run it wherever you think it's on.' The objective is that if we win the ball in our half, let us be in their half the next time we play. So they said, 'Oh right, is that what you meant? That's fair enough.'

There's another thing to consider: how much do you tell a player what to do? And how much does a player do what he's told to do, as against what he thinks is right? The trick is to be able to adjust and think on your feet. And that's been

a battle for all the teams I've been involved with. How much do you give them and how much do you make them decide for themselves? If I err on any side, I don't mind admitting that I err on the side of making them think for themselves, rather than giving them too much information. It's their game. It's the little things that they do themselves that will break down the opposition. So if you are comfortable, work away. If it's by everything that the coach says, that's easier to defend against.

LUKE FITZGERALD: I didn't feel overwhelmed by the information I was given for the New Zealand match. I just felt there was maybe a bit of confusion between players and coaches as to what kind of style we wanted to play. We were poor, we let ourselves down. That's what made Enfield so important – a sense of direction came out of it.

DECLAN KIDNEY: We had Padraig Harrington in with us at Enfield and he was brilliant. He said one side of your brain is the organizational side and the other side is the artistic side. He talked about going with your first instinct, as against being too methodical in your thought process. And in hindsight, we overloaded the organizational side against the All Blacks. You can overcomplicate games.

PAUL MCNAUGHTON: Padraig Harrington talked for two hours. There was a resonance between an Irish team who had come close a lot of times and Padraig Harrington, who had done the same. He had finally started to win majors and he talked about what it took.

At the end of two days, we were on the same page. When we left we knew what we *thought* we were going to do. And then we were going to work at that. We all felt there was a much better mood, a better focus. But you don't win a Grand Slam because you accept that the Munster lads play for the green jersey as much as the red one.

RORY BEST: Declan is very good at putting his point across without maybe you realizing it's his point. It's a very good managerial thing. You feel in the end that it was as much us that drove it as him. But I suppose he got exactly what he wanted without telling us, 'This is what you're doing.' That's a big skill and not many have it. He has it in abundance.

RONAN O'GARA: It's hard to describe it, but Deccie has a way of connecting people. From then on, there was a new code of honesty in the team.

DECLAN KIDNEY: When it came down to it, were there that many boils to lance? There were a few – like there would be in any relationship. But they enjoyed it. And I thought, 'We have a chance here.'

PAUL POOK, STRENGTH AND CONDITIONING COACH: When we met up again before the Six Nations you could sense that the camp was a happier place. The atmosphere in the gym was very positive. The banter was superb – they thrive off each other. My job is to work with provincial fitness coaches to have people in optimum physical shape for a collision sport played at high intensity. They're all very focused on getting the best out of themselves in the gym. Some were born strong and powerful, like Stephen Ferris. Others have dedicated huge time to get that way. Some struggle to stay big.

Our gym at the Killiney Castle Hotel had a bare feel to it so Declan was keen that I give it an Irish flavour. I went looking for posters and pictures, things to brighten up the walls. It was a Sunday morning and I came across this indoor flea market nearby with loads of little stalls. One guy had a couple of prints of old rugby teams. He brought out his folder and he said, 'Look, this is the Ireland team that last won the Grand Slam.' I bought it and I framed it, put it up in the corner of the gym. I spent the afternoon doing up the room – old pictures, recent ones, a Muhammad Ali poster, anything I thought would give the place a lift.

In the evening, I invited Declan to see the room. When he saw the picture of the 1948 team he said, 'Let's write something above it – "The Greatest Irish Rugby Team – So Far".' Most of the players knew Ireland hadn't won a Grand Slam for a long time, but maybe they wouldn't have realized just how long ago it was.

ROB KEARNEY: The Grand Slam was never spoken about during the Six Nations, but going back to Enfield, when we split into the different groups each one said that our goal for the season is to win the Grand Slam. Nobody was afraid to say it. Although we weren't publicizing it in the press, we all knew we were capable of doing it.

DONNCHA O'CALLAGHAN: After Enfield Kearns pushed on as a leader in the team. It's all about gaining respect – and he had it from then on. You'd walk on broken glass for him now.

RORY BEST: Enfield was important but driving back home I wasn't sure if things had changed much – even after all that had been said. But when we met at the start of the Six Nations it was like almost a new place. As early as day one it felt fresh. There was a buzz around. It felt like the sort of atmosphere that had been there two years ago, when we nearly won the Grand Slam – only a bit better again. There was a training squad of thirty-eight and I think everyone believed they had a chance of being involved.

After the talks we'd had as senior players, I knew we were going to be playing it slightly differently – more straightforward. I could see all that in December – we'd spoken a lot about the game plan – but it was hard to see where it was going to change off the pitch. It's one of those things where you're not quite sure how

Declan did it, but straight away it just felt like the craic had come back in. You'd go down to the team room and where previously there would have been nobody there – or only a couple – now suddenly there were ten or a dozen people sitting around chatting or playing table tennis.

We were also drawing confidence from the fact that we knew how we were going to play it. For forwards it's a simpler game when there's a bit less thinking involved. When you're driving at a team late on, you know it's just a case of getting yourself back up, getting around the corner again and working harder. As opposed to thinking, 'Am I in the right place?' That's grand in the first ten minutes of each half when you're fresh and you're always looking for space. But sometimes you just have to have a mentality of, 'I'll not be beaten here. I'm going to get up and I'm going to keep going, keep supporting the lads.'

So in the seventy-fifth minute when you stick your head out of a ruck you know exactly where you're heading. You don't have to gather your thoughts – you pull your head up and you go. In essence, the game plan was challenging us as forwards to show exactly how fit we were and how much mental toughness we had.

PAUL O'CONNELL: The easier you can make the way you play, the fitter you can appear – and the more you can use your fitness. You need to be planning across the pitch. So if we get to this point, quickly, *this* is what we're doing next. But if we get there slowly, then we're going to do it a bit differently. So I know, every time I'm getting up, where I have to go. Deccie's strength isn't in teaching that – we had to drive it. But he'd be very good tactically in knowing what it takes to win matches. And that's the first and foremost thing a coach needs to have. You can be technically brilliant – but you need to know what wins games first.

JAMIE HEASLIP: I felt like I didn't have any ownership of the way we played before. This time, we had our system, but nothing was set in stone. Everything was up for discussion. He wasn't saying, 'It's my way or eff off.' It was, 'This is my way, but we are trying this system out and if you feel something could be done a little bit differently, then fine.' You're not being dictated to.

DAVID WALLACE: Deccie let the team boss it more, in terms of the way we wanted to play. That works better on the pitch because we're the guys making the decisions

GRAND SLAM

out there. We felt we needed a more direct approach to build intensity into the game in the forwards and tire them out and create space for the backs, rather than just being a set platform to give ball to the backs.

LUKE FITZGERALD: For players to really buy into something they have to actually believe that it's going to work. You obviously have to put a certain amount of trust into the coach, into what he wants to achieve, but at the same time you really have to believe that it's the right way to play. And if you have no input into how you are playing the game then at times that can be hard.

What I thought was most impressive about the coaches was they knew all the ins and outs of the game plan they were trying to put in place. They could give you an answer straight away. But there was certain flexibility in all those systems. The game was never going to be exactly as you planned – there was always that flexibility where we could change. And that's what made it so effective.

JAMIE HEASLIP: What Rob said in Enfield stood the test of time. And when we met up again before the Six Nations there was a bit of a different vibe.

ROB KEARNEY: There was a bond, a togetherness. It's about hunger, doing it for the teammates around you. If you want to make the tackles, you will. And for me that was the biggest thing that got us through the Six Nations. There was trust, belief, confidence.

PADDY WALLACE: Something that was slightly lacking in the squad before was an identity and a culture. You roomed with your best mate. You didn't mix too much,

‘ **After Enfield Kearns pushed on as a leader in the team. It's all about gaining respect – and he had it from then on. You'd walk on broken glass for him now.** ’

you weren't forcibly thrown into a room with your opposite number or anything – and that's what Declan did. He roomed you with somebody in your position from another province. It's not that friendships weren't developing already, but it sped things up. He roomed me with Brian and then with Ronan. I found that we were closer, as a squad, than we had been in previous years.

MARCUS HORAN: Even before we had Heather, our daughter, I had found it hard over the years being in camp. Being away from home for so long wasn't easy, but this year it wasn't so much of an issue. It was a good place to be, in the company of the lads.

PETER STRINGER: I had never experienced the feeling of not being in an Irish squad since I started. When I was dropped at the World Cup it put all these questions and doubts into my head, as a player and as a person. It was not a happy time for a lot of us out there. I was questioning my whole belief in the game. It was a strange, surreal couple of weeks and I didn't really know what to do with myself.

I just wanted to get back playing. I remember running onto the pitch in Glasgow for Munster once the new season started and I needed that so much. I thought, 'I'm actually pulling on a jersey again and I'm respected enough by people to be playing out here.' I made a conscious decision that I didn't want to just drift away. I still wanted to achieve things for my province and my country. It was about looking at myself and seeing what I needed to do to get back to where I was. I spoke with a lot of people, a lot of coaches. I said, 'Can you analyse me as if you're an opposition coach? What do I need to do better?'

Over the years fellas had said to me, 'You're not going to have it for ever, you know.' You hear it, but deep down you don't fully appreciate what they mean. Then things happen to you and the realization hits home.

RONAN O'GARA: It's true me and Peter are not especially close but I like the guy and professionally we'd be close. I admired him hugely. He was kicked in the teeth and a lot of people would have shrunk and faded away. But he reinvented himself and came back a stronger and far better player. You have to admire that. He talks more. He thinks more about the game. He offers an awful lot more to a team now than he ever did. You could not but be impressed with the way he fought back.

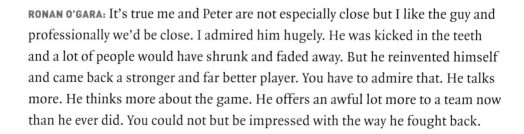

PETER STRINGER: I came into the Six Nations camp and there were three scrum-halves – Tomás, Eoin [Reddan] and myself. You could wreck your head wondering what way a coach is thinking until he makes a decision. I hadn't been selected for the autumn internationals – I was sitting at home watching on television. But it was a time when I'd been given a chance to play for Munster, around the time of the All Blacks game in Thomond Park. I was happy to be playing and I was staying positive.

We went in for a week's training before the France match and he was naming a twenty-two at the end of that week. I trained quite hard and quite well. I know that probably doesn't have a massive bearing on the way things are going to go but you try to remain as positive as you can, right up until the final minute. You're nervous, but you try not show a defeatist attitude and let negative thoughts creep in. You're thinking, 'If I can just get in for the first game I could stay there.' Because generally there aren't too many changes to the Six Nations squad after that.

We went down to the team room and there was a projector and a screen showing two squads – one had thirty players who were to come back training for the France match the following week and the other was the Ireland A squad. I was scanning for my name and it was there in the senior squad. There were only two scrum-halves listed so I knew then I was in the twenty-two. That was a happy time for me, seeing my name up there. I was looking forward to getting back the following week, seeing if I could complete for a place in the team, working hard towards that. That was the next target.

DECLAN KIDNEY: Brian played through those November matches without ever being fully fit. He got injured a week before we played Canada. The captaincy had to be decided again for the Six Nations and I said to him, 'Well alright, you put yourself out to play in those matches and I don't want to take it off you because you're not fully fit.' We didn't have a match again for another two months, so I let him get fit. He was enjoying his rugby. He wanted to carry on. So I asked him to stay on as captain. We had ten days to prepare for the France match. There were several tight decisions but I was picking fellas on where they were playing for their provinces and where they were comfortable. People talked about the selection of Paddy Wallace at centre but that was an easy call. Paddy was playing twelve for Ulster and he was playing well.

BRENDAN GALLAGHER, *DAILY TELEGRAPH,* **3 FEBRUARY 2009:** Ireland have sprung a minor surprise by pairing Ulster's Paddy Wallace with Brian O'Driscoll in the centre for their opening game against France at Croke Park on Saturday. Coach Declan Kidney could have opted for Luke Fitzgerald or Gordon D'Arcy – both regular partners of O'Driscoll at Leinster – but instead has chosen the 29-year-old Ulsterman who has been in fine form this season.

TOMMY BOWE: I was never sure of my position. I was over in Wales and a lot of guys back in Ireland were playing well. When it got called out that I was starting I was relieved more than anything. Relief that I hadn't lost the jersey for doing something wrong. That was big to me. I was thinking back to the last time I played France – the time I got dropped. I didn't want to think about it, but I still had that thought in my head: 'These guys again!'

My dad loves to be in the position of having tickets. The prospect of getting an extra load of tickets nearly brings him more delight than me being on the pitch. I sent him a text saying, 'I'm in! I'm in!' He sent me one back saying, 'Get all the tickets! Take them all!' You're given four complimentary tickets but you have the option of buying some more on top of that. There are people who have been great to me over the years back in Monaghan and for him it's nice to be able to say, 'Listen, Tommy's playing on Saturday and he'd love you to come down and watch – there's a couple of tickets for you.' So then he has to decide who gets them …

RORY BEST: It was another one of those calls when he'd asked me to go and see him. He said he didn't know if it would make me feel any better, but he didn't care which one of us started. It was a toss of a coin – but he'd gone with Jerry this time. I could see where he's coming from – but no, it didn't make it any easier.

JERRY FLANNERY: I was delighted to start, but when it's so close between myself and Rory, it's very difficult to say, 'I have the jersey now.' You're constantly on edge.

RORY BEST: If there was a bit less competition and you were starting every week you'd maybe enjoy it a bit more but you've got to take a step back and take a less selfish point of view on it. You looked at the Ireland bench and you had a lot of serious, toss-the-coin calls. You looked to your left and to your right there was quality all around you.

I was in with Denis. He was after getting a call too but he was in a different boat. He hadn't played much rugby, because of his injuries, and there was a big threat in Alan Quinlan getting onto the bench ahead of him. So Denis wasn't feeling as bad.

PADDY WALLACE: It was the first time I was selected to start a Six Nations match. At home to France – that is pressure. Eddie never considered me as a centre. Declan slagged me the whole week, every time he passed me: 'Well, how's Surprise Selection? See you at team meeting.' 'Oh, it's yourself! Surprise Selection again.' It relaxes you, but you're very aware you have been handed a massive opportunity. And at the back of your mind is that pressure that if you slip up, you may not get the opportunity again.

GORDON D'ARCY: When I got picked in the twenty-two I was genuinely surprised. It was a big gamble on his part. I had only just come back from nearly a year out injured and played in a club match for Lansdowne. I'd worked very hard to be mentally ready for playing rugby again. I wasn't starting against France, but I was ready to play. I felt I was as prepared as I possibly could be.

ROB KEARNEY: The day after the team was picked – Tuesday afternoon – I was running back from a ball in training and Riff [Alan Gaffney] was standing behind me. I tripped over him and banged my ankle. I knew I was in trouble straight away. I was in a bad way.

JAMIE HEASLIP: Jesus, he was on suicide watch for forty-eight hours.

ROB KEARNEY: I was on crutches on Wednesday evening and I was starting to worry whether I would be fit for the Italian game, let alone France. I couldn't speak highly enough of Brian Green [physiotherapist] for those two days. When Brian sees an injury, he just rubs his hands together. He loves it. He thinks, 'This is where I come into my own.'

A couple of times that week Greeny came into my room in the middle of the night, at half-two and five o'clock in the morning. Thursday came and I got a little bit more hopeful. But on Thursday night the ankle was still black, blue, yellow and massive. I was doing my fitness test the next day.

BRIAN GREEN: People think the hard guys on the team are all the Munster guys. But Rob is hard, he's very hard. I was with him on the Thursday night and his ankle looked terrible. Next thing Paul O'Connell walks past and says, 'You're not actually thinking of *playing* are you?' And Rob says, 'Yeah, I am.' Paulie looks at the foot and goes, 'You're a maniac if you play with that.'

PAUL O'CONNELL: It was probably a silly thing to say, but I just didn't want him to think that he *had* to play. I was half-thinking he might feel under pressure. He's a bit old school, Kearns. He's a bit special.

BRIAN GREEN: We've lived with these players day in day out for years and you get

to know them on a few other levels, not just 'What's wrong with your ankle or your shoulder?' In dealing with these people and their bodies, you need them to be honest and forthcoming when they have something wrong with them. Our strength as a medical team is that we are quite personal and personable with them. We do try to have fun with them – and we do.

PAUL O'CONNELL: Brian is a massive part of the camaraderie and when someone has a serious injury he's really, really good. But he can't answer a straight question. If you ask him, 'What colour is that shirt you're wearing?' he won't answer. He'll say, 'Let me ask *you* something …'

BRIAN GREEN: These players want to represent their country, no matter what. And sometimes there's a balance with an 80 per cent Player A and a 100 per cent Player B. And you can only report to the powers that be, 'Look, we think he can go fifty minutes. He could break down – we're not sure. You also have to factor in other games that are coming up. Over the years now, the players have begun to trust us and if you're honest with us, that only helps us to get you better, quicker. But if you aren't fully honest with us, it makes it a bit more difficult.

They're very open with us now. They've almost gone in the other direction – now they come to us before there's a problem. They'll say, 'I'm starting to feel something.' And that's good.

CAMERON STEELE, PHYSIOTHERAPIST: I'm the traditional physio in that I would do nearly all of the hands-on treatment, Brian does specialist rehab. Psychology is a big part of it. Declan is quite the sports psychologist and I'd like to think that we are helping him in that regard. He would certainly come in and try and get a handle on where certain individuals are at mentally. You get a feel for each individual. You know each animal and how he reacts to certain situations. If John Hayes says he's got a problem, then you know it would have anybody else in hospital.

DR GARY O'DRISCOLL: John Hayes is astonishing. The man never complains. Often I'd go round the changing room after a match, sweeping up the various injuries, and I'd see John in the corner and he'd just look at me. The poor bloke would

be in absolute agony with his ear. I'd go over to him, stick a needle into it and stitch it back together.

JOHN HAYES: My ears are pure solid. For some reason, they don't bend. They get bangs in scrums and they bust open.

I won't wear a scrum cap, not a chance. I taped my ears alright for a long time, but I hated it. Imagine the state of me running around the place with a scrum-cap on – my big mallet of a head. I don't like wearing anything. The less I have on the better. My jersey is all I want on. There's always something aching someplace. A shoulder one week, an elbow the next. Someone will have walked on it, but if it's not too bad – play away.

CAMERON STEELE: You're putting fellas on the field that in an ideal situation would not be playing, so part of it is dispelling a fear factor. That player knows he's not 100 per cent and you've got to get it into his head that he's safe to play, that he's not going to do himself any harm – he can go out there and perform for his

country. In the back of your mind you're questioning yourself – is that the right
thing to say? So you've got to rely on your clinical judgement and your experience
to be certain that you can safely put them on the pitch.

ROB KEARNEY: It's always good when medical staff tell you, 'Listen, it's going
to be hell sore, but you won't do any more damage to it.' It is sort of reassuring.
It was bloody sore but once I knew that I wasn't going to do any long-term
damage, it was a case of just suck it up for a week and take the pain.

LES KISS: It was all on the line in the French game. Everything that had been
said at Enfield, the spirit we now had it in squad – it was all being put to the test.
The moment of truth was coming and our balls were all on the line because the
French had threats everywhere. We had searched into ourselves and challenged
each other and come up with something. France was going to be the defining
game for us.

CHAPTER 4
FRANCE AND FRIENDSHIP

It is Friday, 6 February 2009, the night before Ireland's opening match in the Six Nations championship, against France at Croke Park. In room 288 of the Shelbourne Hotel on St Stephen's Green, Paddy 'Rala' O'Reilly is lying back on his king-size bed, his head against the pillows. He is regaling his audience with another tale of Inishbofin, the island seven miles off the Galway coast which he has adored since he first visited in 1976. In the nervous hours before they take the field for their country, the Ireland players like to listen. Even if they pretend otherwise.

'I might have told ye this one before, lads,' he says. 'It's about a great fisherman – Willie Lavelle is his name. A good friend. At the height of me drinking time I was in the Doonmore, staying with Mrs Murray and drinking me loaf off. Whiskey, brandy, everything. There was great music and all that, but Willie was going fishing the next morning at six o'clock and I said I'd go with him. Now I struggled up to bed about four, lads ...'

Donncha O'Callaghan and Marcus Horan put hands to their mouths and yawn.

'Next morning, Willie is outside me door. "Are you right, Paddy Reilly?" So off we went in a currach. I was in bits, lads. In bits I was. We were out a good way, now, and he was doing the lobster pots. I was still in a terrible state, so Willie says, "I'll bring you back in, Paddy Reilly – you waster, you." I said, "Jaysus, Willie, is there anywhere you can just leave me off and come back for me?" He says, "There's a little island there, Inishgoirt. I'll leave you there now and come back for you." So I got out of the currach and struggled, like Robinson Crusoe, onto the little beach. There was a bit of a gale blowing at this stage ...'

O'Callaghan and Horan begin to snore.

'So I crawled up the beach and hit the grass. Turned over on my back and just conked out. Next thing I heard this screeching. It sounded like that Hitchcock film, *The Birds*. I looked up and about a foot above me there were seagulls flying around. I went, "Jesus!" and they all scattered. But lads, I was telling Willie when he collected me and he said, 'You're lucky, Paddy Reilly – because they would have gone for your eyes. They just see an animal. So if you ever do that again, lie on your stomach." I was lucky there ...'

O'Callaghan and Horan are now stretched out on the floor, snoring uproariously. Suddenly, they 'wake' with a start ...

'Oh sorry, Rala!' says O'Callaghan. 'What were you saying there?'

GERT SMAL: The first game, we said we wanted to approach it as a final, because it was so important to start well. If you don't have those butterflies there's something wrong with you. You can have nerves, but you must never be scared.

Once we got to the ground I was pretty calm. You've done all the hard work, you've had the best preparation you can have, and there's not much more as a

coach that you can do. You can say one or two things to one or two players and activate them. But you don't want players thinking the coach needs to tell them what he expects before they are activated. The players must have what they call self-actualization. You want players to have inner motivation. Then you know you're working with quality players.

BRIAN GREEN: The way I see it, there are two types in the dressing room right before the game. There's the pillage and carnage type, who'll be saying, 'We're going to effing kill them! Let's smash them!' Then you have other players who are more direct and technical, a bit more calm. 'We'll smash Chabal when he comes around the fringe. We'll go phase after phase. We'll keep going at them – and we'll score. And then we'll do it again.'

It's all about mental imagery. Every sports psychologist will tell you that. See yourself do it – then you'll do it. Our two leaders are like that. Some of the others just sit there and don't do anything at all – David Wallace doesn't say a word before we go out. Some of them will vomit right before the game. There are others who can cocoon that pressure, use it – and be calm.

These people, in a lot of ways, like routine. A lot of them read certain passages in books. One or two read a book they've had from school, maybe some message, some phrases. Jamie Heaslip has done it now, we've noticed. Andrew Trimble would read the Bible. Flannery would be another one. You don't ask to look.

JERRY FLANNERY: It's something my mother gave me when I was at school – the Miracle Prayers of Divine Mercy. Before every game I sit down and give myself ten minutes to pray, because I find it centres me.

‘ **Some of them will vomit right before the game. There are others who can cocoon that pressure, use it – and be calm.** ’

BRIAN GREEN: Sometimes, before they go out, they'll yell for something. Two minutes before they go out on the field they'll shout 'I need tape!' They'll say their wrist is a bit sore. Some of them ask for crinkle-cut tape, a stretchy tape that adds no support at all, but they've got to have it on their wrist. So you do it and they think, 'I'm now ready.' Ronan, two or three minutes before they go out, or even right after the anthem, starts yelling for tape. He never wears that in practice. But right before he plays matches he likes to have that on there.

DR GARY O'DRISCOLL: Probably as a team doctor you shouldn't become passionately involved. But because of my family and our tradition, that was always going to be the way for me. Brian is my second cousin. Barry is my father – he won four caps at full-back – and his brother John O'Driscoll got twenty-six caps.

You end up working with the lads so much that instead of patients they become your friends. I don't think anyone will forget the day we played France at Croke Park in 2007 and Clerc scored in the last minute. I remember being in that dressing room and in my eleven years with the Irish team it was the worst moment. That tore the lads to pieces. Grown men of 120 kilos were sitting there, destroyed. This time, we owed them.

> **Ronan, two or three minutes before they go out, or even right after the anthem, starts yelling for tape. He never wears that in practice. But right before he plays matches he likes to have that on there.**

STEPHEN FERRIS: It was my Six Nations debut, eighty thousand at Croke Park, a massive game for me. I'd never played against Sébastien Chabal before, but Declan said, 'We picked you because you're playing well for Ulster – just enjoy yourself and do exactly the same for Ireland.'

In the changing room Paul said to me, 'I've never beaten France.' He was desperate to beat them this time.

BRIAN O'DRISCOLL: I couldn't believe Paul had never beaten the French because I'd beaten them in three of the first four times I'd played against them. But then again we hadn't won against them in seven years. I didn't really have to say it – there was an overriding feeling that we'd really been done two years beforehand and we owed them one. I thought, 'Let's just play as I know we can and get into them.' The big thing was giving the crowd something to cheer about because there had been question marks about the atmosphere in Croke Park.

We went out with a confrontational attitude: 'We want to take you on up front – if you want to match us, let's see it.' The Munster forwards have been involved

in a lot of those sort of games, but they couldn't have done it that day without the ability of the other players from other provinces. I'm not taking away from them at all, but this team was about the different parts coming together.

PAUL O'CONNELL: In their pack they had no Ibañez, no De Villiers, no Pelous. It was very different to the teams we had played down the years. It turned out to be a really good game. We did some great stuff, they did some great stuff.

ALAN FRASER, *DAILY MAIL***:** The French attacked everything, from everywhere, to the point of lunacy. God bless their lunacy.

RONAN O'GARA: They were running at me – but 100 per cent of teams attack the 10 channel. That's one of the core values of rugby. Teams go there for their first phase. Then they go around the corner. When they look at me I'm not big physically so it makes perfect sense for them to go there. Every team is going to go after me. They try to batter you, they try to limit your influence in attack.

JOHN O'SULLIVAN, *IRISH TIMES***:** The French served notice on fourteen minutes with a wonderful sweeping move. Florian Fritz bounced O'Gara to make the initial bust, Maxime Médard's chip and Fulgence Ouedraogo's hands kept the move alive and when it was swept to the far touchline, Sébastien Chabal regathered a bouncing ball and Imanol Harinordoquy crossed in the corner. Lionel Beauxis posted a superb conversion from the touchline.

CAMERON STEELE: Coaches vent a lot of their frustration to us physios down the mike. They're really helpless up there and we're their conduit to the players. So when you concede a try like that – in what was a huge match for us – you're going to get it. But the players know generally what's going on so when coaches are trying to give you chapter and verse on what they have to do, you just summarize – or you ignore it. You'll get a coach coming down the line saying, 'Tell them to get stuck in!' Now if I went to Paul O'Connell and said, 'Gert says ye need to get stuck in', then I'd have my head in my hands. So you don't say that. The coaches are just venting anxiety – deep down they know we're not saying it all. So what do you actually say to Paul O'Connell? 'Water or Powerade?'

RIGHT: Ronan O'Gara tries to bring down Imanol Harinordoquy: '100 per cent of teams attack the 10 channel'

LES KISS: They had talked before the match about going all-out in attack so we knew they would run from everywhere if they thought it was on. And that's what happened. They had deep support lines, lateral support lines, they were keeping the ball alive and they were dangerous all across the park.

We knew what was coming and the players had worked hard on dealing with it but in rugby it doesn't matter how much you want to plan something: you can't design things to have perfection. That was the bottom line when I first spoke to the players. I put it in the final slide of my presentation: 'SHIT WILL HAPPEN.' I said, 'The thing that will define is how we find a way to deal with it when the shit happens.' France were playing brilliantly, but we hung in. We came back at them.

This game is imperfect but you get the odd perfect moment. For me as defence coach, we had one a couple of minutes after that first French try. We wanted to push the boundaries on line speed and decision-making. Our system isn't one thing or the other – we don't come up soft, and we don't come up hard all the time, like Wasps or Wales. We want to be able to see opportunities and shift it when they're there. It can be a shooter sometimes – and in that first half it was

Brian. There was a scrum in the middle of the park and the French nine shaped to move it back into the line, to Beauxis. Brian sniffs it and he moves. He lines up Beauxis – whack! Brilliant. It's about decision-making, it's about choosing the right moment – and everyone backs the decision that Brian has made. They're hunting hard, they're in their faces, searching for more opportunity. One moment like that can drive a lot of confidence about the system. And when you get it working once, then they start to feel it again. They start to trust.

A second O'Gara penalty has cut the France lead to 7–6 and the match is thirty-two minutes and thirty-five seconds old when Jerry Flannery brings the ball behind his head at lineout twelve metres inside his own half. Ireland have four men in the line – Horan, Heaslip, Hayes and O'Connell. They have spent many hours studying how France defend off a four-man lineout – which is narrowly in midfield. They know there will be space to exploit if they can get around the thirteen channel and they have a power play to bust the French defence. Flannery is grimacing from concentration and, at 33.37, he propels the ball into the air.

JERRY FLANNERY: They know I'm not going to throw it to Marcus and I'm not going to throw it to John Hayes. So it's going to be one of the two jumpers – Paul or Jamie. It's all down to speed. I see Paul loading himself, moving down so that his next movement is to spring straight up. He's like a coiled spring and the split-second I see him start to accelerate up I have to throw it hard and fast, to a certain point in the air. So I'm watching Paul – and Paul is looking at the ground, he doesn't want to give anything away. The second I see him move up, I just zip it. I know he's going to be there to take it if the throw is good. When you get it right, it's a very, very difficult lineout to defend, because it's all about speed.

PAUL O'CONNELL: Harinordoquy gets his hand to the top of my chest. But Jerry's throw is an absolutely perfect, top-of-the-jump throw. Even though Harinordoquy has competed well, his hand doesn't get near me. It's a great feeling in that moment – we've won that mini tactical battle. It's a really, really good lineout – off the top, out to Tomás.

O'Leary, as instructed by Gert Smal back in August, is standing five metres away at ninety degrees from the jumper and takes the pass low, with Flannery already upsides him and on the charge. O'Leary's pass is swift and sweet and with the backline moving the ball comes beautifully into the hands of O'Gara. Unchallenged, he skips two men in the line and finds Wallace.

DAVID WALLACE: It was a set play. Hit me and truck it up. I carry it and give it back to the winger. Tommy was coming on a line behind me so as the cover closed in all I had to do was give it to him.

The move has been rehearsed all week and Bowe knows the next link in the chain: he fires it ten yards left across the line to the advancing Kearney.

ROB KEARNEY: The move was identified to get the right winger to come up and in on me. For him to try and make a read – but they defended it completely differently. I felt they were drifting quite hard so I tried to get on Jauzion's inside shoulder and then Tommy ran a great line off me.

TOMMY BOWE: I made a break then down the left and got an offload from Rob. I kept running at them and one of them was pulling me back but I kept going. They had cover straight in front of me so I turned.

Bowe spins around and sees O'Driscoll three yards behind him, gesturing with a hand for him to hit the ground and recycle. He goes low and waits for O'Driscoll to reach him. There are five blue jerseys closing around two men in green. O'Driscoll dives over the top to protect the ball, Bowe is spreadeagled on the turf and the ball comes loose as four arriving Irishmen hit the ruck hard. O'Driscoll stretches out his right arm and pushes it back and O'Leary, the last man in, crouches low to collect and then ships it fifteen yards right, to O'Connell.

PAUL O'CONNELL: We had busted them miles over the gain line. Normally when it goes to the touchline we truck – hit in with the forwards. But when you've made a twenty-yard break all bets are off.

BRIAN O'DRISCOLL: The big thing for me in the whole play was Paulie in midfield, his understanding of the need to shift it to Rog. His decision there was either going to make or break that try. No disrespect to forwards, but they understand going forward – and there aren't many second rows out there who would have that awareness to make that pass. A lot of forwards would have tunnel vision, just truck it up. He just understood. There is no one like him for trying to take a team on confrontationally, nobody to match him. But the right call there was to shift it – and he made it.

RONAN O'GARA: I took it from Paulie and I just saw a space – a fella hitting a hole. So I just put it there. I didn't know it was Jamie at all.

I was in shock, in awe of how well he did. What a step! I didn't expect him to finish it from there.

As Heaslip slaloms through the gap the French full-back Poitrenaud is calm, his stride unhurried.

JAMIE HEASLIP: Breaking the line was easy, because it was a prop and a second-row that I went through. Rog just put me through the hole, but then I saw Poitrenaud ahead. I thought, 'I ain't gonna outrun this chap.' So I started to make a beeline to the left. He was legging it and I thought he'd overran it – so I stepped back inside. Once he had to turn side-on to me and I stepped, I knew he was in trouble. The other guy [Médard] came across and I just had to bash him, basically. I was so close I just had to hold onto the ball and barrel over. My keg took me over the line. Somebody said I was like a barrel of beer being thrown into a cellar. It was a class feeling. You get up and the first faces you see are your team mates and they are going ballistic.

RONAN O'GARA: I was in shock, in awe of how well he did. What a step! I didn't expect him to finish it from there. I think all of us were thinking, 'Jesus! In fairness, Jamie, that's outstanding.' Poitrenaud underestimated him big time – and Jamie scorched him. It was very impressive, a forward doing that – it's a huge piece of skill. And essentially what is needed at this level is tries – you're not going to win by penalties any more.

MERVYN MURPHY: When Jamie went under the sticks I was burning up inside. We worked hard on it all week and they are the moments you get satisfaction from. Massive buzz. That try gave us huge self-belief.

TOMMY BOWE: As soon as Jamie scored Ronan turned and ran back to me. I was thinking, 'Hold on a sec – you're right beside Jamie, are you not going to go celebrate with him?' Then a couple of other guys came over to jump on top of me because of my break. It was a confidence booster for me. You could see there was something good in the team, a good camaraderie. France had been brilliant, but I thought, 'Ah, we're back in it!' They knocked over a drop goal right before half-time so it was seriously close and a great game to play in.

A couple of minutes before that, Chabal made a twenty-yard break and I took him down. I knew Rob had him covered but our backs stick together. If there's

any sense of trouble you're going to make the tackle. I landed right on his studs and thought I'd broken my rib. I spent the rest of the match trying to breathe.

CONOR O'SHEA, RTÉ ANALYST: It is truly incredible that we are leading this game 13–10 at half-time. But look at France over the last couple of years – in the last quarter of their games they have actually tired. They've weakened in the last quarter – so you stick with them.

GEORGE HOOK, RTÉ ANALYST: Conor, if you want to roll with the punches, if you want to use that strategy, your team has to have huge morale and it has to be very brave. Now this team, like all Kidney teams, has high morale and is very brave.

JERRY FLANNERY: We look at our work rate as one of our strengths. We believe we are fitter than the opposition. I'd got a stinger after about twenty minutes when we were defending on our line. I hit a nerve in my neck and got numbness down my arm. I could feel it getting worse at half-time, everything started to lock up

in my neck. You don't want to be the guy that misses a tackle because you're too proud to go off so I wasn't sure how long more I was going to last.

I went out for the second half and a couple of minutes into it Paul called another lineout ball on himself, outside their twenty-two, and won it easily off the top.

RONAN O'GARA: I got it from Tomás and I had Brian outside me. People talked about the pass afterwards, but there was nothing to it. It was a routine pass.

BRIAN O'DRISCOLL: I was just setting the ball up, I was just giving us go-forward. It was early in the second half and we needed to get some territory, to build some phases. I got into Beauxis, Jauzion left me, I got a bit of a hand-off to Beauxis and I was off. Then Malzieu came across but I knew when he was booting it over to me that any step inside and he was gone. I scored a try in 2005 against France in Lansdowne from a bit further out, which was very, very similar. I handed off Freddie Michalak, ran across, Heymans came running over and I stepped inside

him. I shot straight for the try line not knowing where Dusautoir was because he's such a tackle machine he could have been there any second. Maybe I could have helped Rog for the conversion by bringing it right under the sticks, but I wasn't worried about that, I was thinking about getting it down immediately. I was thinking, 'I could get hit from behind here', so I went down.

GERT SMAL: When Brian is in that form, he's incredibly dangerous. I was happy for him, because even though he has been there and done it, he always wants to improve and he has a massive will to win. I'd like to see all the Ireland players with that attitude. When you see the amount of time he puts in in front of a computer, looking at his own game, you understand why he's such a special man. When you work that hard, you deserve to be rewarded and it was a great try for him.

BRIAN GREEN: What Brian says is, 'I will work on what I'm good at.' Because if you constantly try to work on the things that people say you need to improve on, in the end you probably don't go anywhere.

RORY BEST: At half-time I was in the indoor warm-up area because I'd been told I could be going on early. Jerry wasn't right and after Brian scored his try I was told, 'Get ready – you're coming on.' It was great to get on the pitch but about a minute later their 10 kicked a ball over me and into the corner and it bounced up perfectly for Médard. Coming into a match cold is an absolute nightmare. You're running everywhere, you just can't get your second wind. You're trying to chase the game because everybody else is into the pace of it.

About five minutes after that they hit a drop goal and they were within two points of us. I've been in teams where you've been comfortably ahead and then it all starts going wrong – but we weren't panicking. There wasn't that sense of, 'Oh no, they're all over us.' It was very calm and very collected. We just said, 'We'll have to step it up another gear here to get this win.' In that game, it struck me that we had the capacity to win things.

PADDY WALLACE: In the first half I had broken out from their twenty-two and I got split just above my eye. I was blinded but we had to keep defending for another two minutes before I could get off the pitch. I got four stitches, but it didn't stop the bleeding. They took me off for good in the second half and it ended up that I needed sixteen stitches. It scared my kid, looking at me.

PAUL O'CONNELL: It was a good physical game and as a pack we were enjoying taking them on. We were happy to pick and go, pick and go, to keep going at them. That was something we didn't do much of before. They're a good side and you might go back a metre sometimes, but maybe the next time you try it'll be quick and you'll make three or four metres.

DENIS LEAMY: I think we're lucky. We've got some very instinctual players who do stuff off the cuff. They do things in split-seconds without thinking. They see half a gap and in that split-second they can bust a defence. Guys like Drico, Wally, Tomás – and D'Arce.

GORDON D'ARCY: I was on a few minutes, we were getting closer to their line and the forwards were gaining those inches and yards, sucking in their defenders. The closer we got to the line they were just collapsing in and then you needed more numbers around the ball. We had four guys and I was just screaming for the ball. When I was calling it, Dusautoir was on my inside and when it came to me from Tomás he drifted to my outside. Your instincts take over at that stage. You trust yourself to make the right decision. He was trying to hedge his bets, to attack the space out wide. I just stuck it under the wing and got a good step. Two more defenders came in on me but I was only a couple of yards short and I turned and got across the line.

LUKE FITZGERALD: You could see from everyone's reaction, after D'Arce scored, how much it meant to all the people around him. We were so delighted that he was back and competing at the highest level. It was a year of frustration and I'd say he was anxious, really worried about his injury. We were as well. There were rumours, there were whispers. It didn't look good for him.

ROB KEARNEY: Myself and Gordon went to the same school [Clongowes Wood] so he mentored me a bit when I was coming through the system. Even before I got

into the Academy I would keep in touch with D'Arce. I was just really, really happy for him. He went through so much pain in the year off. A year is a long time. What do you do with yourself when you're not playing rugby? You go insane. There was a massive release. It was a special moment for him.

GORDON D'ARCY: It was strange. After I scored the try, running back for the kick-off, there was a moment of clarity. I thought, 'It's all finished now, all done, all behind me – the injury is gone.' For your really close mates to be the guys picking you up off the ground is brilliant. Somebody got the photograph, framed it and sent it to me – it was waiting in the hotel when we got back. And if you look at that photograph, Brian is there, Rob is there, Luke is there, Jamie's there – he's the guy that's first in. Looking at it, you can see they're so happy for me – it means as much to them as it does to me.

It's very hard to articulate something like that, it's a very personal moment. The three or four seconds when you're being yanked up off the ground and everyone slapping you on the head and going, 'Well done! Great try!' – that's fantastic but that's not it. It's the ten or so metres when you're running back to the half-way line, when you're on your own and you have a few seconds for your own thoughts – that's when something clicks inside you. I suppose that's when the reality kicks in. The people who sent me the picture, maybe they don't understand just how symbolic the whole gesture of framing that moment was for me. I'm a big believer that what you do in your life makes you who and what you are – and while you'll always remember the good times, you should never forget the bad times either.

It's a nice reminder. It's up on my wall now and I can look at it and go, 'Yeah, if I came through that, I can do anything.' Me and Brian, we've grown up together. We played against each other in schools rugby. He was happy for me and when Brian says something to you, it means a lot. Your friends are there in the good times and the bad times. That was a good time we could all share.

DECLAN KIDNEY: When Gordon scored the try the whole team was thrilled for him. Two days of meetings in Enfield didn't lead to that warmth, the camaraderie that people saw then – it was always there. And not alone is it a great try, it's a try scored by one of our own, who has fought his way back. Does it get any better in rugby? Not for me.

LES KISS: They got it back to six points, with a penalty – and then straight away
Rog made it a nine-point game again. Three minutes left and they were great
minutes for me. They proved we were going to be a hard team to beat, to break
down – because you could actually find a soft moment there, if you wanted to.
The clock went red, France could have scored and it wasn't going to cost us the
match. But the French team became devoid of anything, they couldn't work it out.
The boys, they just refused to concede – their willpower was immense, just the
mentality and the belief. I thought afterwards, 'That's a good sign.' Going down
in that lift, coming down through the bowels of Croke Park, was a wonderful,
beautiful feeling. Gert was rapt. He was saying, 'This means so much to me.'

GERT SMAL: I was very satisfied, specifically with the lineouts and with our whole
game management. If you go wide all the time, your backs will fall out of the bus
in the second half. If you play with your forwards all the time, your forwards will
fall out of the game. So you have to have a balance. You need to know what you
want to do with your pack to maximize their energy over the eighty minutes. I was
actually amazed how the team stepped it up. It was powerful to see that. You can
only do that if you have special players in the team. And like I've said, there's not
just one – there's a few of them.

PADDY WALLACE: Gert is a man of few words, but after that game he spoke to us.
He was emotional, he told us how proud he was of us. You could see what it
meant to the coaching staff as a collective unit.

JERRY FLANNERY: No matter how much you believe in what you are doing, in the
game plan you have put in place, the result does reinforce your belief in what
you've done. You think, 'This *does* work.'

BRIAN O'DRISCOLL: There's no doubt about it, we played our best rugby in that
game. Personally, I felt good to be hitting some form. I didn't worry too much
about what people might have been thinking; I always thought I had it in me.

I think if I'm honest, I probably wasn't as professional as I could have been
for a couple of years. I could have been fitter than I was – put it that way. I think
that comes with a degree of immaturity and a love of life. I'm talking four years

ago, I'm not talking now. I think there is way more than just your rugby life, there's your general outlook and what's going on in your head, what shape you're in and what's going on with your extra-curricular life.

I probably didn't have the contentment that I have had in the last two or three years and that goes a long, long way. It's no coincidence. I'm more driven as a result of knowing what I want and having what I want. It's a nice place to be at. It gives you a freeness to go out and completely enjoy and focus on your rugby.

PAUL McNAUGHTON: After the French game I was getting messages from guys I played with – David Irwin, Ollie Campbell, Fergus Slattery – saying we could win a Grand Slam. Some former players don't want the players that follow them to win anything. That's a fact. But these guys were genuinely excited and the thing that amazed me was how quickly people started talking about a Grand Slam, after one win. That frightened the life out of me.

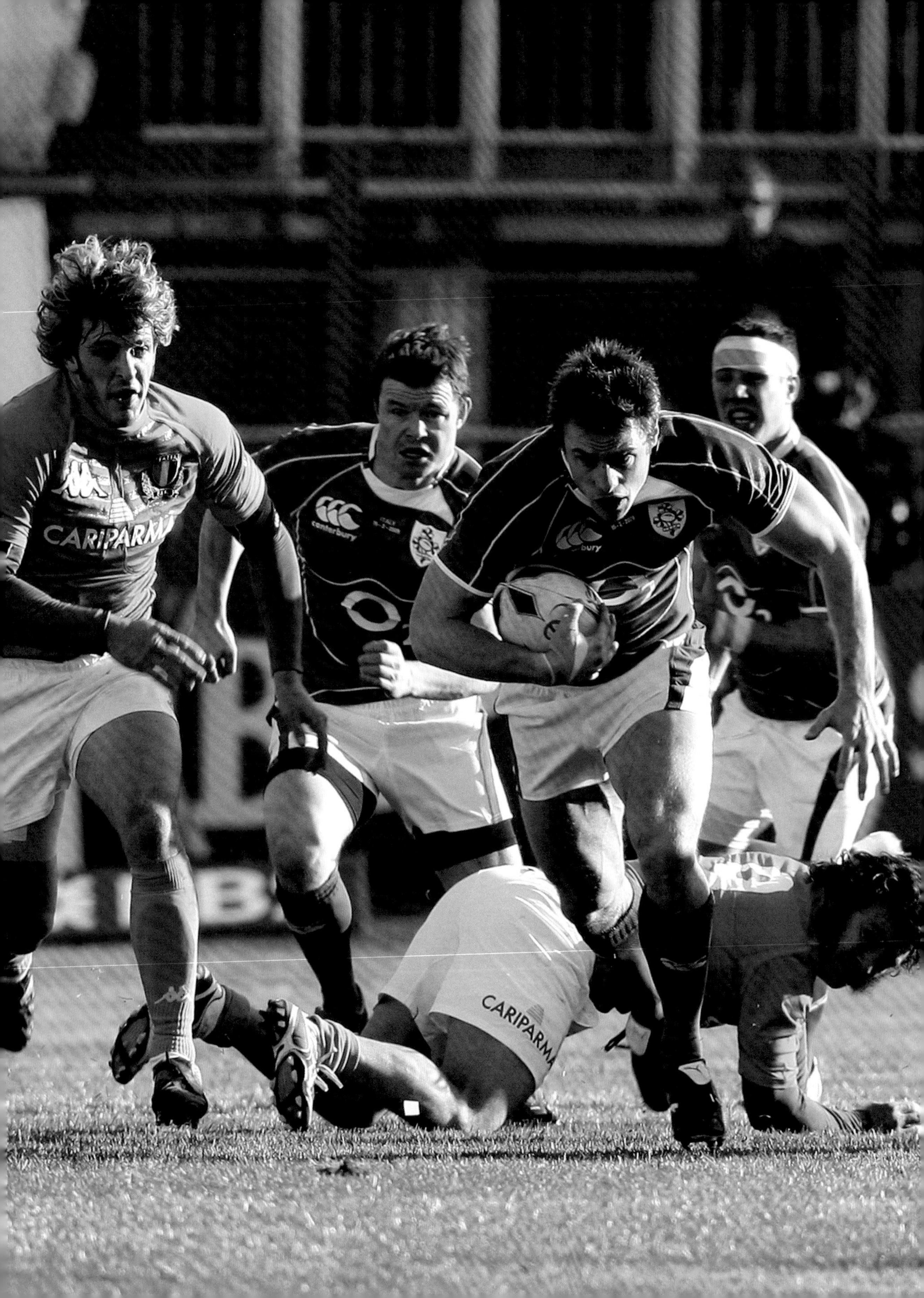
CARIPARMA
canterbury
CARIPARMA

CHAPTER 5
RUMBLE IN ROME

Italy, next up for Ireland, had been beaten 35–11 by England in a dire match at Twickenham. That margin flattered England, who benefited from the first-half nightmare endured by Italy's emergency scrum-half, the great openside flanker Mauro Bergamasco. Kidney named an unchanged side for the match in Rome.

In the *Irish Independent* two days before the match, the journalist Peter Bills spoke to Massimo Cuttitta, an Italian prop forward throughout the nineties. Cuttitta felt the Azzurri would be up against it, but offered them one ray of hope. The Irish scrum, he said, could be vulnerable on the loosehead side and Marcus Horan was likely to suffer against Martín Castrogiovanni, Italy's tighthead.

MARCUS HORAN: I didn't see the article, but some of the lads told me about it. It said I was the weak link of the team and that the scrum was going to be in serious trouble.

DONNCHA O'CALLAGHAN: I'm friends with Marcus, more so than just teammates. I knew the agony he went through over that. He was hurting, it really upset him. But I saw it as rallying call for the whole pack. I thought he was questioning the whole lot of us, not just Marcus, because we're a unit and we stick together.

MARCUS HORAN: I don't think I got the caps that I've got too handy. I think I was there for a reason and it became just a motivational thing for me, it drove me on. The guys that I'm up against are bigger and heavier than me, so I'm up against it straight away, but I've got Donncha behind me. The lads all read the article and I think they were gutted for me. I wasn't going through it on my own.

LEFT: Tommy Bowe's intercept try put points on the board for Ireland after an aggressive Italy took a 6–0 lead in Rome

PADDY WALLACE: I was worried about retaining my place for the Italy match. Gordon had come on against France and scored a try and I'd been off the pitch a couple of times. We run teams in training and on the Monday it was to be the same team up on the board. But you still can't read anything into that. So I was really relieved when I stayed in.

TOMMY BOWE: Everybody's family turned up because they all like coming out to Rome. Everything is set up for a fall. You go for a cup of coffee and you bump into half of your home town, all with their sunglasses on and a pint or a glass of wine in their hands, telling you what a great weekend they're having. It's all very nice – but you're trying to focus. You're thinking, 'Jesus, we have a match here.' We were expecting Italy to be physical and we knew they were going to come at us hard straight from the kick-off.

STEPHEN FERRIS: Usually I would be slightly tense, but I had no nerves going into the game at all. I was feeling strange. In the warm-up my legs felt heavy. I started worrying then: 'Why am I feeling a bit lethargic here? I should be pumping!'

PADDY WALLACE: Right before the whistle we went into a huddle. Rog said, 'These boys will come at us, but we have to deliver here. Nobody has talked about it, nobody has mentioned it, nobody's saying anything – but it's time that as a group of players we started believing that we can win a Grand Slam – and it starts today.'

RONAN O'GARA: What clicked in my head was that we had blitzed Italy a couple of years before when we were going for the championship and Denis Hickie spoke really well the night before. I had a feeling that this could either be a game we'd barely win, or else we could go for it and set down our standard for the rest of the tournament.

GERT SMAL: I played a lot of club rugby in Italy so I know they can get really emotional. I told our players, 'They will definitely come out hard in the first couple of minutes. But we will be ready.' The comment about Marcus was just pre-match talk by people who are not close to the team, people who haven't got a clue what you're busy with. I don't care what people say beforehand.

> **‘ Masi caught him hard around the neck with a straight arm. Rob was going at such a pace that his legs went right from under him. ’**

All I care about is that the pack is well prepared, that we know what they're going to throw at us.

DR GARY O'DRISCOLL: In the first minute, I was right by the side of the pitch and Rob Kearney was running a fantastic line at great pace. It was one of those moments where you can see what's coming next. Rob was fifteen yards ahead of me and he was going to beat the cover. Then I saw Masi coming up and I started shouting, 'No! No!' I could see it happening before it happened. Masi caught him hard around the neck with a straight arm. It was appalling. Rob was going at such a pace that his legs went right from under him. Players have no control in that situation. They're going at such speed that when their legs are taken out from under them like that you worry not just about the hit, but how they land. I remember running onto the side of the pitch, shouting at the referee and swearing, perhaps not in the most professional manner.

LUKE FITZGERALD: I had the best view of that. I was right next to it, four or five yards inside Rob near the left-hand touchline. I was shouting for the ball, I could see your man coming a mile away. It was incredible, shocking. He should have been sent off straight away. It was only because it was so early in the match that he got a yellow. I thought Rob was gone. He got absolutely milled – his feet flipped out from under him.

JAMIE HEASLIP: He could have hit Rob with a proper tackle and hurt him, but he clothes-lined him. I legged it from the other side and got completely the wrong guy when I came in shouting at him.

DR GARY O'DRISCOLL: When I got onto the pitch and got to Rob he was dazed, he was winded. I got him to sit down so that I could assess him properly. But typical of Rob, he was saying, 'Let me up! Let me up!' And I was saying, 'Stay here! Let me assess you – let me check everything's okay.'

Sometimes players will try and carry on when they shouldn't. Rob is not the biggest player but my goodness he's a tough, tough boy. He shrugged it off. He was telling me, 'Look, I'm not letting this fella get one over on me.' When he was back on this feet some of the lads came up and said, 'Well done, Rob.' It meant a lot to the rest of the team.

The speed and the power in these games just keeps rising – and the guys keep getting bigger and stronger. You wonder where the line is going to get drawn and as a doctor it does worry me. If there is foul play it's got to be stamped on. Tackles like that have to get rooted out of the game.

MARCUS HORAN: When guys are mouthing like he was to Rob, they're probably hiding something, some weakness. It was up to us to exploit it. It was great to see Rob get up and get at them so quickly.

For me there had been a build-up of anger and bitterness over what had been said. The first scrum collapsed and Castrogiovanni looked across at me and said, 'It's going to be a long day for you.' Donncha was going ballistic behind me. He was roaring, 'It's going to be a long day for *you!*' It just rose me, got me going, and the next scrum we blitzed them. I didn't have to talk. I knew I had the support of the boys behind me.

DONNCHA O'CALLAGHAN: I knew what it meant to Puppy in the scrum. Sometimes that stuff can be a good thing because the focus he brought into that game was incredible. He was a standard-setter for the pack.

He gives me everything he has in lineouts – every lift. He never drops his standards. That day I knew I had to give him absolutely everything in the scrum. My shoulder was red raw from being behind Pup and I'll be honest – it should be like that every week.

JOHN HAYES: Everyone was going to back Marcus. No one was going to leave him on his own. Not too long after that first scrum, we looked up and there was your man going off – the fella mouthing about Marcus having a long day. He had a short one. With about twenty minutes to go I saw him coming back on and I thought, 'Did you just take a little break for yourself?'

Some people think they can get a reaction from opposition players by mouthing on. Maybe, after all these years, they've realized they're not going to get a reaction out of me, so they don't bother. Nobody says nothing to me any more. They might have said something before, but I never took any notice of it.

‘ **Donncha was going ballistic behind me. He was roaring, ‘It's going to be a long day for YOU!'** ’

RONAN O'GARA: Hayes doesn't get involved in sledging. He's just thinking of the feed after the match.

TOMMY BOWE: About twenty minutes into it, Brian came up hard around our twenty-two and half the backline got left behind. His defence is brilliant – the only problem is trying to stay with him because you never know when he's going to blitz it. It's up to the wingers to back him up if anything goes wrong. I was still trying to catch up with him when next thing Canale threw a pass across to [Mirco] Bergamasco, it came off him and I was able to follow in, grab it and take off.

LES KISS: They just sniffed it. Because they were pushing hard into certain places, they forced the error. They forced the opportunity.

TOMMY BOWE: I was trying to concentrate and look towards the try line ahead of me, but I could hear people behind me the whole way and because it was a sunny day I could see shadows. I didn't know where they were coming from – I could just

hear them, getting closer and closer. I was thinking, 'Jesus, they're going to get me! Someone's going to tap my ankle!' That would have been typical – I would have landed right on my nose five metres from the line.

I felt someone grabbing the back of my jersey but I was nearly at the line and it was just a case of getting the ball down, getting in on the grass. A couple of years ago I scored a try against Italy at Lansdowne Road and when I was walking back they showed it on the big screen. Next thing the crowd went 'Ohhhhh!' because you could see I hadn't touched it down – so this time I was going to make sure of it. It came at a good time because we weren't looking too good and the Italians were six points up.

STEPHEN FERRIS: It was great, a real forward-orientated game and I was loving it, getting stuck into those guys. Whatever lethargy I had disappeared once the whistle went. We didn't start very well but Tommy's try settled us down a bit.

Then Rog, after all his talk, gets sin-binned and nearly ruins it for us. Ah but we'll forgive him.

RONAN O'GARA: It was poor selection. I tried to kick and I was never going to clear them – so charge-down. Your man [Canale] got the jump on me and I basically tackled him without the ball. It's a natural reaction – it's just panic. I was always going to get a yellow card. They're difficult to play against. They have regressed badly over the years since Dominguez went. They think physical play is the only way. But I played poorly in that first half.

PADDY WALLACE: A few minutes after Rog got binned I made a half-break, and as Brian was coming to clear an Italian player out of the ruck he smacked me on the face. I could feel the eye swelling and filling up with blood. An eye injury had forced me off against France and everybody probably thought I'd opened up the old wound, but it was the other eye. An injury you'd expect every three years I got twice in seven days.

DR GARY O'DRISCOLL: Paddy was a like a boxer who'd got the edge of a glove into the eye. It closed straight away. Myself and Cameron were under awful pressure to get him back on. I took him under the stand and we got the stitches in and

stopped the bleeding. He comes straight back out and I'm examining him on the side of the pitch with four or five minutes to go in the half and there's some choice language coming over the airwaves. The boss is saying, 'Get him back on!' That's the polite version. It's very stressful and Paddy is going, 'Let me back on! Let me back on!'

PADDY WALLACE: After I got stitched Gary said, 'Jesus, I don't know if you can actually see out of that eye.' And I said, 'Yes I can – I'm grand! I'm grand!'

DR GARY O'DRISCOLL: The hardest part of the job is when you've got to tell players as dedicated as ours that they can't go back on the pitch. Unless you have actually been there I don't think you can properly appreciate it. The noise. The atmosphere. The intensity of the game and the pressure on the players – it does end up coming on to you as medical team.

You don't have time to fully assess. You have thirty seconds, a minute at best. Sometimes play is still going on around you. The easy thing, always, is to let the player go on. But you know that if you do – and he misses a tackle – then it's going to come straight back on you. You've got to be very careful, because if you start taking players off too early on a regular basis, you will lose their confidence. The coaches won't be happy either and they'll get somebody else in.

So Paddy is standing on the sideline, looking at me with his one good eye, begging me to let him back on: 'Please, doc, let me on! Please let me on!' But he can't perceive depth. He won't be able to see somebody on his right-hand side. He could let himself down. He could let the team down. I said, 'Paddy, you can't go on – you only have one eye.' Over the radio they were going, 'We'll make this decision at half-time!' I said, 'No, we can make this decision now. This eye is not going to open.' Paddy was gutted. He had been playing fantastic rugby and he had taken the physicality of his game to another level. It was tough on him.

PAUL O'CONNELL: I thought the Italy game was really good. We went wide two or three times at the start and threw the ball on the ground. We shouldn't have been doing that anyway – we needed to take them on straight up, first and foremost. The ball should have been in Wally's [David Wallace's] hands, running over someone. Just before half-time, we hammered away with the most unfancy play of the whole tournament. We went backwards by about fifteen metres at times but eventually got a hole through Stevie Ferris.

STEPHEN FERRIS: We knew we had to come away with some points. The forwards kept working on it, coming around the corner, coming back, seventeen phases, picking yourself up off the ground, let's get back into it, round again, one more

'The hardest part of the job is when you've got to tell players as dedicated as ours that they can't go back on the pitch.'

– come on! It's a mental game and if you can tell yourself to do it, you'll do it. We didn't think we were good enough realigning in our attack formation against France so that was in the back of my head. Get up, get back in position, make yourself available, we need options here, give an option.

Strings was on and I just screamed at him. There were a couple of options outside me and he heard me from a good bit away, coming around the corner. I took it and just ran as hard as I could at a half gap and Luke followed me in. I left it up for him and he did the rest. I remember lying on the ground, sucking in a bit of air, watching Lukey going under the posts. Then somebody just grabbed me and lifted me up. Back into it. Soon after that was the half-time whistle and then we just kicked on from there.

JERRY FLANNERY: People had lost the run of themselves after the French game – not within the squad, but supporters and journalists. They were were saying, 'This is it, they'll win the Grand Slam.'

I knew Italy were going to put it up to us early on, but we work so hard on our conditioning and we know we're going to be fitter than other teams as the game goes on. We want to show them that we're only getting going here – we try to mentally break them. I thought it was going to be ugly rugby for fifty minutes and eventually the tries would come. That's how it panned out.

Ireland led by just 14–9 at half-time, but second-half tries from David Wallace, O'Driscoll and a second for Fitzgerald gave them a 38–9 victory. Fourteen of those points came in the final five minutes and they would prove crucial as the championship came down to the wire. There was a debut off the bench for Tom Court, the Ulster prop with poetic tendencies. After two games, Ireland led the table on points difference from Wales, conquerors of Martin Johnson's England in Cardiff. They hadn't played especially well, but they had answered O'Gara's pre-match urgings and maintained their momentum. the next match was thirteen days away, against an improving England.

MARCUS HORAN: We went out that Sunday night in Rome and myself and Donncha came back to the hotel in a taxi with Rob. He was a bit the worse for wear – and he was excited. He kept saying to us, 'We're going places, lads!' And it was true for him.

CHAPTER 6
RALA'S STORY

John Hayes loves his cup of tea after a match. I always put a red apple on John's towel in the changing room – not a green one, it has to be red. A guy working for French TV in Paris noticed this once. He asked me why I put the red apple there. I said, 'Jesus, that's a very good question. I've no idea.' I've been doing it for years, but I don't know why I'm doing it. I don't know if he eats it. He probably says, 'Not another bloody red apple from this eejit.' But he's so nice, John. He wouldn't ask you why he's getting the apple.

For me it all started nearly thirty years ago in that bar there. You see over there? Through that door. Paul Joyce and Barry Coleman were about to take over the Terenure College first team and I just happened to be standing at the bar there, having a pint. Or two. They says to me, 'We want you to be the bagman.' Now I had just finished playing, but I didn't remember there being a bagman. I didn't even know what it was, but they said they reckoned I'd make a good one. I made a few phone calls. You know Peter Smith, the St Mary's coach? I rang his da up – his nickname was The Rainbow. He was doing Leinster and he gave me a few tips. So it sort of went from there.

People call it a job. It's not a job to me, it's a love. Now it's not all wine and roses – there are hard days, sad days. I couldn't do this without the help of so many people in so many different areas. They know who they are.

I don't think I'd last that long in any other sport. Because they mightn't be the same. I know my lads. I call them 'my lads'. Which they are, I suppose. They're never ... they wouldn't be fazed by anything, in my opinion. So that actually makes you try even harder, you know? To have what they require. They'd do anything for you. They're very generous with everything, especially their time. They all muck in.

I'm always nervous. Always butterflies. There's always something that's not quite right. But if it affects the boys, they'll always let it wash over them.

'Don't worry, Rala, I'll get on without it.'

The night before a match, they all arrive in my room in their own time. You could nearly set your watch to them. Drico is always last. Leamy and Rory Best come in two or three times during the night. Some stay a minute, some of them are there for two hours. Peter Stringer? He's in and out about ten times. They chat away themselves. I don't really listen – it's their time. When they arrive I say to them, 'Is this a social call, or do you have business?'

They come looking for sweets. Jesus, if you haven't got them you can wrap up your blanket and go home. Wine gums, fruit gums, maybe the odd éclair. Rory Best, he calls me O'Reilly, you know? I'd put out a packet of fruit gums, but I'd have another packet hidden.

'O'Reilly – is that all the sweets you have?'

'Yes, Rory.'

'I don't believe that, O'Reilly.'

He'd sniff around and he'd always find it, no matter where I'd put it. You could put it in the toilet cistern and he'd find it.

I put the shorts and socks neatly on the bed – forwards one line, backs one line and then subs. So here's what happens. Wally comes in, with Stringer.

'Jesus, the carpet is very slippy there, isn't it, David?'

'Jesus it is, Stringer.'

There's nothing wrong with the carpet. Then they jump, like they're diving into a pool, all over the bed. The shorts and socks go up in the air, scattered to the four winds. And then they start picking them up and putting them into different pairs. There's two sizes of socks, you see.

'You'd want to get that carpet fixed, Rala.'

Then you settle it all up – and the next thing Marcus comes in. Gone again. Denis Hickie brought a banana skin into the room once and threw it on the floor.

'Oh, is that a banana skin I see there? Whoops …'

Quinny [Alan Quinlan] wasn't in the twenty-two in the end but to me he's sort of another Claw, you know? One of his things is, am I for Munster or for Leinster? Who do I support? He comes up with the most crazy ideas. The latest one is, Ronan and Brian are hanging by their fingers on a cliff's edge, with a thousand-

feet drop into a volcano, and my other half Dixie is over there and a guy has a shotgun at Dixie's head. I can save one of the guys – but only one – and Dixie will be spared. So who will it be, Ronan or Brian?

'Come on, Rala, I want an answer.'

'Ah come off it, Quinny, how can I answer that?'

'I need an answer, Rala. I need it now!'

I'd yap me way out of it. 'Connacht's my favourite team, Quinny. Shur we go to Connemara all the time.' In the old days they put this electrodes thing on me. Rob Henderson used to be at it then. 'Munster or Leinster, Rala?' Great character, Hendo.

So that's the crack. If you were driven demented by it you wouldn't last a week. Usually, on the night before a match, I'm not finished with them until midnight. You'd miss the lads who don't come in any more. Claw. Keith. Gaillimh. Jeremy Davidson. Paddy Johns. Denis McBride. Mo Field. A whole list of them. I miss them all. I'm sort of sentimental like that. They're always slagging me about it. I consider them great friends. It's an honour to know them. Because a hundred people could do what I do. Maybe two hundred. I'm just lucky that I'm there.

‘**They come looking for sweets. Jesus, if you haven't got them you can wrap up your blanket and go home. Wine gums, fruit gums, maybe the odd éclair.**’

'I'd never felt
such exhaustion
in all my life.

CHAPTER 7
ENTER ENGLAND

England travelled to Dublin as 3–1 underdogs, but for those not caught up in the hoopla over a potential Ireland Grand Slam, there was persuasive evidence that Martin Johnson's team were on the turn. Kidney named an unchanged side, but made one alteration to the bench, with Mick O'Driscoll coming in for Malcolm O'Kelly.

After a training camp in Cork, the squad returned to Dublin, where a member of the players' entertainment committee, Jamie Heaslip, received a phone call which resulted in him being mercilessly derided for the rest of the tournament.

JAMIE HEASLIP: This thing has been blown out of proportion.

LUKE FITZGERALD: Not at all. It hasn't been given enough publicity.

JAMIE HEASLIP: Let me put it on the record. I was phoned up by Brian's mate Damo. He said, 'Would you like Snow Patrol to come in to ye guys on Thursday night? To walk round and say, "Howya? How's things?"' No one said they were going to come in and play a private gig.

ROB KEARNEY: Surely they wouldn't have come all that way just to say hello.

JAMIE HEASLIP: This is gospel! In my infinite wisdom I thought, 'It's overkill. We're going to see them on Sunday night and we'll probably be going backstage – so we'll leave it off till then.' But I quickly realized I had made a grave mistake. Weeks later, John Hayes was still going through me over it. I mean, he probably doesn't even know who Snow Patrol are.

DONNCHA O'CALLAGHAN: It was just complete naivety by the fool. He let down the entertainments committee badly, so we made him write a letter to Snow Patrol. We didn't want them thinking, 'These fellas have been offered a private concert and they prefer the cinema.' After that he wasn't allowed to make a decision until he'd run it by two other guys. We booed him any time he walked in.

We enjoyed watching him squirm. The craic in the camp was good all year. The only problem we had was that at one stage Rala got a bit cranky because Deccie and the lads were messing around with the itinerary. Rala prides himself on making sure the players are looked after and the itinerary for the next day would normally come around to you around eight o'clock. But for a while the coaches were having these massively long meetings and the itinerary was down the list of priorities. Poor Rala nearly had a stroke. He would be outside the door, wanting to know the time of training for his itinerary. He'd come around to your room at eleven, apologizing. We were loving it. I was saying, 'This is ridiculous, Rala. It's eleven o'clock!' He'd say, 'I'm very sorry, I'm *so* sorry.' Then I'd be ringing Leamy going, 'Rala's on his way. Tell him this is just not good enough.'

Rala has all these little lines that he comes out with, like 'Even a cat can look at a king' and 'What comes out of the cat is in the kittens.' At the start of the Six Nations he started putting one of his lines at the top of the itinerary. He called it 'Rala's Thought of the Day'. It sounded like a great idea but by the time we got to the week of the England match he was saying to Ger Carmody [team services manager], 'I can't think of a bloody thought!' He had no more thoughts left.

PADDY 'RALA' O'REILLY: The players like the thoughts of the day so they told me to keep them coming. I was asking various people if they had any for me. I went up to Ruth Wood-Martin [nutritionist] that Thursday and I says to her, 'Ruth, have you any ould saying for tomorrow?' She gave a good one about a tomato and the next thing I heard Brian was after coming out with it in the press conference. I think he had a bet with one of the lads but I'd say the journalists were baffled. I says, 'Jaysus, what will they make of that?'

OWEN SLOT, *THE TIMES:* Well into his tenth Six Nations Championship he may be, but Brian O'Driscoll's eve-of-battle one-liner yesterday is further evidence that the Ireland captain is sharp as ever after all these years. Asked about

Martin Johnson's qualifications to run the England team, he paused, then said: 'Knowledge is knowing that a tomato is a fruit. Wisdom is knowing not to put it in a fruit salad.'

PETER O'REILLY, *SUNDAY TIMES:* Boredom clearly got the better of him. In O'Driscoll's defence, this was his fifty-first eve-of-Test-match press conference, which is around fifty more than any man should have to sit through. They are mind-numbing, where captains and coaches have only one concern – not providing opponents with any motivational fuel.

❛**Knowledge is knowing that a tomato is a fruit. Wisdom is knowing not to put it in a fruit salad.**❜

MARCUS HORAN: Everyone was expecting us to win and the way people were talking was a potential disaster for us. You could easily fall into that trap. They have serious players. We always had that fear of losing at home, of losing to England at Croke Park, because we are guests on the pitch and we want to do it justice.

TOMMY BOWE: Before the England match Declan stood up and explained the importance of it. He talked about the great work that the guys had done two years before, on that massive occasion. I was down there watching it and I was blown away by the atmosphere before the anthems and then by how Ireland played. All Declan had to do was just remind us it was a huge, huge match – the last time we'd play England in Croke Park. He talked about the people who fought for us to get that opportunity. He said, 'This is more than just us a team – it's a massive game for our country.' My dad was saying, 'Jesus, half of Monaghan's coming down – any chance of a few more tickets?' My phone was jammed up for two days with people's texts, reminding me of what it meant to them. I hadn't heard from some of them for ten years.

ROB KEARNEY: I was so nervous. More so than for any other game. Being a spectator for the last game in Croke Park, it seemed a monumental occasion. And I think as well, the feeling of the whole of the country was, 'This is not a great English side – we'll beat them easily.' In fact, they are a really good side. For me, it turned out to be the toughest game of all of them.

TOMMY BOWE: We were massively up for it. France had beaten Wales the night before which meant we were the only unbeaten team left in it. Brian didn't need to say much at the captain's meeting that night. He asked if anybody wanted to say anything. Paul spoke and what he said stuck with me. I thought of it again after the match. He looked around the room and he said:

Think about what it's going to be like after the match. Picture yourself in the changing room. Picture Willie Bennett coming in. He makes the best cup of tea in the world – as long as you've won. He'll put about six spoonfuls of sugar in it. That cup of tea is nice and hot, you're just sitting there absolutely wrecked and you're drinking this hot tea – and it tastes absolutely divine. It's the best cup of tea ever.

Picture yourself taking off your strapping, knowing that you did your job. Picture

yourself sitting there listening to Declan telling us that we've given it everything – and we've won. We've beaten England.

You're doing this so that you can have a moment like that. Whatever you might have in your head as the perfect scenario after the game – picture that. And know what you have to do to make it happen, to make your picture real. You go out there and you work your ass off for the team.

So I pictured myself in the changing room after the match. But in the end the picture I had in my head wasn't like the reality.

JERRY FLANNERY: You grow up wanting to play for Ireland. I don't normally sing the national anthem, I get too emotional and I worry that I might lose my focus. The first time I sang it was at against England Croke Park in 2007. I thought, 'If I'm ever going to sing it, I'll sing it here.' I was lucky I was on the bench that day because I spent twenty minutes trying to get my head right after it. I wasn't going to make that mistake again.

PADDY WALLACE: The minutes before the match weren't as tense as I thought they would be. When *God Save the Queen* was about to start, I was standing beside David Wallace and I leaned across and said, 'Wally, would you mind if I sang along to this?' A little joke.

DAVID WALLACE: It was probably the first time I've ever laughed in a line-up before a match. Normally my heart is pumping and I'm really nervous. I was hoping the cameras didn't catch me laughing.

GERT SMAL: Each team tries to expose you in different ways, asks you different questions. England were physical, they hit very hard.

❛I don't normally sing the national anthem, I get too emotional and I worry that I might lose my focus. ❜

> **We took them on up front. I sound like a broken record, but that is the most important thing to do against England.**

TOMMY BOWE: It was a battering match – one of the toughest games I've ever played in. It wasn't pretty – it was never going to be. They were always going to give us a physical match so that no matter the result, they could look at us and think, 'You played England today and you know all about it.'

PAUL O'CONNELL: We didn't produce nearly as much as I thought we could. But the thing is, we took them on up front. I sound like a broken record, but that is the most important thing to do against England. In the years after they won the World Cup they lost a lot of leaders and others like Vickery and Tindall were in and out. But they are a really good team. The plan is to take them on and provide quick ball for the backs to have a cut. As forwards, we didn't provide enough good ball. And when we did, they didn't have a good cut.

LES KISS: When you're a coach up in the box, looking down on it, you're thinking, 'Where's it sitting, this game?' And where this game was sitting was that England were an extremely difficult team to break down.

DECLAN KIDNEY: We had a lot of ball, but we weren't making any inroads. Is that poor attack – or do you acknowledge the fact that England only conceded two tries in the whole Six Nations?

MERVYN MURPHY: My biggest worry in the middle of a game is, 'Do I have Rog's tee?' I keep having this nightmare that I'll lose it. In my second year I was walking down the tunnel for the second half of a match, minding my own business, when he stuck the tee in my face and said, 'You forgot that – you eejit!' I was in a state of shock for five minutes.

RIGHT: In a tight defensive match, Tomás O'Leary makes a rare clean break

When you go onto the pitch with the kicking tee or a water bottle, the better coaches will give you a concise message for the players. But often, when you get to a huddle, they're being given the same message already. Somebody's getting lambasted by Paulie.

Fifty-two seconds have elapsed in the second half. Ronan O'Gara, standing over a penalty kick thirty-eight metres away, glances up at the posts. The score is 3–3, but on another day Ireland would be six points clear: O'Gara has already missed two penalties.

RALPH KEYES, RTÉ CO-COMMENTATOR: It's straight in front of the posts practically – and you would think it's not the most difficult for a man of his kicking class.

MARK TAINTON: Croke Park is not the easiest place to kick at. The wind seems to come one way, bounce off the stand and turn around. Ronan always practises kicking straight down the middle of the posts. Otherwise, with a wind, you're guessing too much. Looking back at that kick, you can see from the expression on his face that he thinks he has nailed it – and then it comes off the sticks.

RONAN O'GARA: It was a good strike – I was certain it was over. I was as shocked as a lot of people in the ground were. The first one was a good strike too, but it went left. The second one was a terrible strike. This one, I turned back thinking it was over. Why did it happen? I wouldn't be one for putting it down to 'one of those days'. Was I confident standing over every ball? Yes, I was. Did I get nervous? No, I didn't. Would I have been nervous five years ago? Damn right I would have been.

The greatest thing I learned out of that was that you have to differentiate your training sessions from a match. I kicked as well as I ever have that week in training and maybe I didn't make the transformation mentally. Some days it's so easy; against England I struggled, and I didn't have the answers. That's because I'm human – we're not machines.

I was disappointed, frustrated, questioning myself. But that's only natural. It will happen again, but if you want to stay at the top and constantly get picked these things can't happen very often. There's pressure on me, but pressure from myself. I'll always remember the reaction of people when I came home. They were shocked. They were saying, 'Are you okay?' I can tell you, I'm a lot stronger than that.

MARK TAINTON: As kicking coach, you do feel it, watching on. You spend a lot of hours together working on the technique. I tell him, 'If you miss a kick, it's gone. Every kick is your first kick. No kick is different, no matter where you are on the field.' His technique has been so good for years, it's proven.

PADDY WALLACE: I just thought, 'He'll kick the next one.' Some days as a 10 you can do everything that you normally do and the ball doesn't go between the posts. There's no real answer why. I never thought he would hand the reins over – not Rog, not at all. He will always back himself. He has massive confidence in his own ability and I never once expected him to turn around and give me the nod.

❛Was I confident standing over every ball? Yes, I was. Did I get nervous? No, I didn't. Would I have been nervous five years ago? Damn right I would have been. ❜

Their defence was excellent – Mike Ford had them well drilled – but we kept going at them and then Brian kicked a great drop goal to put us ahead.

LES KISS: Brian's a dangerous player, he can punish a team in a lot of different ways. If I was the opposition defence coach I would be trying to close everything off around him. You've got to choke his source. If you're in his vicinity and he's got the ball, you're going to try and put him to deck every time. He cops some big knocks and he makes some big tackles. A few minutes after that drop goal he came out of the line and nailed Riki Flutey. And straight after that, Flutey took him out.

BRIAN O'DRISCOLL: I should have shipped it, it was a turnover ball and we had numbers outside. But I thought, 'Let's play territory – get it down there.' It was actually a half-decent kick, which is unlike me.

CAMERON STEELE: There was head-on-head contact and when we reached him he was on the ground with his eyes shut, in a lot of pain. Gaz [Gary O'Driscoll] had just left to join Arsenal so it was me and Mike Webb over him. The blow was to the temple, which is not a good area to take a heavy impact. There can potentially be internal bleeding and we needed to establish if he had lost consciousness for any period of time. I said, 'Brian – what just happened? Who hit you?'

Brian, when he's pent up and in the zone, can react quite aggressively to an injury. He was immediately remonstrating that he knew exactly who'd hit him and what happened. He was saying, 'He caught me late. Do we get the penalty? Have they stopped the clock?'

RIGHT: Shortly after recovering from a head-on-head tackle by Riki Flutey, O'Driscoll chips towards the line. A split second later, he was taken out by Delon Armitage, and required further treatment

BRIAN O'DRISCOLL: I had this piercing, splitting headache. Physically I felt okay, I knew I wasn't goosed – I just couldn't shake the headache. Sometimes you just need five minutes and you get it back. I took a couple of painkillers out on the pitch.

CAMERON STEELE: As soon as you know he's with it and focusing on the match you are quite reassured, but your concern then is that he's not deteriorating over the next five to ten minutes, that he hasn't had a concussive episode. You have to get back on regularly to check that he's still able to verbalize properly and focus properly, in terms of his vision. It isn't easy verifying that with Brian because his vision is shocking for a guy at his level. He can't read the scoreboard.

Two or three minutes later, he was down again. He chipped ahead, got blocked by Delon Armitage and took another nasty blow, directly to the sternum. More than a month later he was still getting pain from that. Again he was remonstrating with me that he was hit late – and was the ref giving a penalty? He's got pain in his head, his neck, his shoulder and his chest. We've got the coaches in our earpieces saying, 'Can he function? Will he be okay?' And we were saying, 'Look at him – he's in a lot of pain.'

The team sees their skipper down and if he comes off at that stage in such a tough match, it's going to be a serious blow. But when a player is still in pain from a head injury you have serious concerns. If that head pain persists, you can't let him stay on the field. The coaches were relying on us to make the call. It's a very complex organ, the brain, and we have to make these decisions in the heat of the moment. We weren't far away from taking him off. We decided to give him a few more minutes.

‘I had this piercing, splitting headache. Physically I felt okay, I knew I wasn't goosed – I just couldn't shake the headache.’

LES KISS: He kept getting off the deck and every time the crowd was lifted. The cheering rose up all around the ground. When Brian gets going, it brings confidence into the team. When he was down, Paul stepped up and showed leadership: 'Our captain is down, guys – this is the play. We're going after them.' We had a penalty for the foul on Brian, but they wanted a try.

O'Driscoll comes back on the pitch, clutching his head, grimacing. O'Gara kicks for the corner. O'Connell wins the lineout and they pick and go, pounding away until a penalty is awarded. Craig Joubert warns that one more infringement will bring out the yellow card. Another lineout. They keep driving. Phil Vickery is all over the ball in a ruck and gets binned. Ireland scrum. One after the other, they drive at the line. Heaslip, O'Connell, Wallace. All repelled.

LES KISS: You felt, watching it, 'Something is going to come from this.'

BRIAN O'DRISCOLL: The boys had been hammering away, softening up the defence. I was standing there, waiting to have a crack. I saw it was Julian White and Nick Kennedy at the base of the ruck and I really fancied my chances against them. I was two yards out and I thought, 'Give me a shot and I'll definitely get over here.' I didn't think for a second that I wouldn't. That's arrogance, but it's difficult for big men like that to get low quickly.

LES KISS: He had been battered twice in five minutes. He was still suffering from a bad headache and he dived head first into contact, low and fast. The pure will of the man came through. It was one of his finest hours.

CAMERON STEELE: It was a try that probably very few other backs in the world could have scored, so it's very difficult then to tell the coach that you're still concerned about his head injury. But whether it was the euphoria of the try or the adrenalin, the pain did subside. It's a relief when you make a big decision and they are okay.

STEPHEN FERRIS: It was seriously physical and I was loving it. I don't really care about my body when I'm tackling a guy. I put everything into it and I'm not thinking, 'How am I going to come out at the other end of it?' It's more, 'How is *he* going to come out?' Big tackles have an impact on games and if you're going

❝ That's arrogance, but it's difficult for big men like that to get low quickly. ❞

to have a massive hit, you have to time it perfectly. I don't run onto the pitch going, 'Right, I'm going to smash everybody today.' Not at all – I just wait for an opportunity to come.

After Brian's try, Tomás put a box kick up over Delon Armitage. I thought, 'I can challenge for this ball or I can absolutely smash him when the ball's in the air … I'll smash him.' As soon as the ball started coming down to him I quickened and hit him just as he caught it – bang. It's about timing – he can't tense himself up to lean in to me and take the force. They were dishing out plenty of punishment themselves – they're a really tough team.

ROB KEARNEY: We had to work bloody hard for that try. Then they came back with a penalty and there was only a score in it [11–6]. It was a tough, tough match and if they had been more disciplined, it could have gone a different way.

DONAL LENIHAN, *IRISH EXAMINER:* Martin Johnson thumped his fist on the ledge in front of him when Danny Care committed disciplinary suicide by mindlessly driving into the exposed back of Marcus Horan, leading to his dismissal only three minutes after his introduction off the bench.

MARK TAINTON: Ronan had missed four and the penalty we got after Care's yellow card wasn't easy. We needed it to make it a two-score game. It was a pressure kick. He nailed it straight down the middle.

Ireland lead 14–6 and the margin does not flatter them. Four minutes left. A huge cheer goes up as Brian O'Driscoll is named the RBS man of the match. People are drifting out of Croke Park. Suddenly, Mike Tindall surges through, Andy Goode kicks towards the corner and Armitage beats Horan in the chase. Goode converts – and the margin is one point. Seven

*seconds remain on the clock after O'Gara restarts. England run hard and spread it wide and
then Leamy, on for Heaslip, kills them off with a juddering tackle on Tom Croft. Match over.*

TOMMY BOWE: We came into the changing room. I was sitting there on the ground
with my legs stretched out, socks pulled down. I couldn't even sit on the bench
I was so tired. It was nothing like the mental picture I'd had. Brian was on one
side of me, Rob was on the other. Brian was in a daze. There was strapping
coming off, there was blood. Paddy's face was still half mangled from the match
before. The forwards were all shattered. I thought, 'People outside will think
we're popping champagne and roaring about the place. They couldn't be more
wrong.' The place was silent, it was almost like a morgue, almost like we'd lost.
Somebody said, 'Did we not win this game?' Then there were smiles. We were
too tired to shout and roar but there was a lot of happiness and a lot of pride.

Willie Bennett came over. 'Cup of tea, Tommy?'

'Ah Willie. I'd love one, please. Plenty of sugar.'

Paul was right. It was a beautiful cup of tea.

'People outside will think we're popping champagne and roaring about the place. They couldn't be more wrong. '

STEPHEN FERRIS: I got showered and changed. I was completely punctured, zapped, wrecked. There's a warm-up area in Croke Park and I went in and slept for half an hour. I'd never felt such exhaustion in all my life.

DONNCHA O'CALLAGHAN: Out of all the things in rugby, that's what I love most – when you've given it everything and you're just sitting in the dressing room with the lads. They are the great days, they're the ones I will always remember. I'll be honest – that hour when you're sitting there recovering is the only truly enjoyable part of the week. When you've won and you're there with your teammates, there is no better feeling. Every joke is funny after you've won.

PAUL O'CONNELL: That game was an arm wrestle – and we won it.

CHAPTER 8
CHANGING OF THE GUARD

Fitzpatrick Castle Hotel, Killiney, 9 March 2009

RALA'S THOUGHT OF THE DAY: Measure twice, cut once *(Donncha O'Callaghan)*

Paddy Wallace had a bad feeling about the Scotland match. Then again, since his call-up against France he had worried about his place against Italy and England too. This time, the axe came down. On the Monday before Murrayfield, he was milling about in the team room when Kidney asked if he could have a word. He thought nothing of that, until he strolled out to the corridor and saw Jamie Heaslip, Jerry Flannery and Tomás O'Leary walking in front of him. They looked at one another and Wallace guessed what was coming.

'Lads,' said Kidney, 'since I started I've talked about wanting to develop a squad. This match is an opportunity for me to select guys who've been knocking on the door – and unfortunately you're the guys who are going to miss out. You're not being dropped. You're not being rotated. It's just something that I feel needs to be done this week.'

ALAN GAFFNEY: You could understand people saying, 'What's this about? We've just beaten England, we're undefeated. What are we doing?' But I had no problem with it. None. As a coaching team we were united on that decision, totally unanimous. If we had made one change, it would have appeared that the player had been dropped. Make four changes and we're just doing it from a squad perspective.

RORY BEST: I was aware that the four guys had been pulled but until you hear the fifteen out of Declan's mouth you don't dare to dream. When you've been

in camp for five or six weeks it gets to the point where you feel it's never going to happen. I had been coming off the bench but I was aware that the minutes had been creeping up on Jerry's side and down on my side. I was thinking, 'Hold on, I don't want it to get into the seventies before I come on here.'

You feel more involved when you've started a game somewhere along the line. I was rooming with Denis and he came in for Jamie. It was a big lift for both of us, it made a difference. I'm sure Strings and Gordon felt the same way.

PETER STRINGER: To be starting again in the Six Nations, it was nearly like a first cap again. I was getting phone calls from friends and family, texts saying 'good to see you back in there'. But the tough bit is still to come. You've to go out there and perform.

JAMIE HEASLIP: The last thing I said to Deccie was, 'Fair enough, you're dropping me – and you know I'm not happy with it. But I'm going to be Mr Positive, don't you worry about that.' We were trying to build a squad mentality, so I had to buy into that. I probably did bitch privately to Rob and one or two others, but I tried to be pretty positive for the whole week. On the day of the game, Deccie pulled me aside and thanked me for my attitude. Which meant something – the fact that he noticed. Most coaches wouldn't have taken the time to say anything.

GORDON D'ARCY: I was talking to Jamie after it and he said, 'They're going to have to put me on at some stage and I'm going to make a massive impact, so he can't not pick me against Wales.' That's the way to react to something like that.

MARCUS HORAN: That Monday night, Christy Moore came out to Killiney and played for us. He'd been in with us a few times before and the last time there was a poor showing of fellas getting up to sing – and all he wants to do is to sing with us. This time five lads sang and they were outstanding. Lukey got up and sang *The Reel in the Flickering Light*. The two of them went at it and I'd say Lukey nearly knew the words better than Christy – he was brilliant.

PAUL O'CONNELL: Deccie saw us throwing it around a little bit in training. He thought maybe people were reacting a bit to the comments that we hadn't played

much rugby against England. He has a good sense for what wins matches and he said, 'We don't need to change what we've been doing.'

DONNCHA O'CALLAGHAN: I've been looking over my notepad – Christ, how many notes did I take on Scotland? It was all about them – watch this, watch that. Yes, it has been a difficult match for Ireland to win down the years. And yes, they have quality players. But, with no disrespect to Scotland, we put so much emphasis on them that we probably talked it into being a closer game.

PAUL MCNAUGHTON: Look, nobody outside the camp wanted to talk about the Scottish game. Even at that stage, everybody wanted to talk about Cardiff. Yes, there was a cautious approach to the games. But in many ways you had to do it, because if you start talking about beating the crap out of somebody, then you are actually saying, 'Let's get this over with and move on to Cardiff.' That was something the coaching staff were not prepared to do. Ireland have been flummoxed so many times at the last hurdle, beaten when we should have won.

> **I spent the next three days feeling like an idiot. But it also meant I had to focus on getting fit, rather than spend the week feeling sorry for myself over not getting picked.**

So the caution that was there was about respecting our opponents – which we always do. Maybe sometimes you go overboard on that. But Christ, it's better than going underboard. Because then you could be out on your arse.

JERRY FLANNERY: We were practising lineouts on the Thursday and I was being the Scottish hooker. The ball came back to me and I grubbered it. I should have left it at that but I started running, trying to score. I suppose I was still a bit bitter about being dropped. Donncha started tearing after me – Johnny Tryhard. I dived and he came in on top of me as I hit the ball. I rolled on to my back and just lay there. Everything seemed to go quiet. I was thinking, 'Oh God! Please let me be able to lift my arm.'

PAUL O'CONNELL: It was completely Fla's fault – nothing to do with Donners. But it was typical of their personalities.

JERRY FLANNERY: Slowly I tried to lift it – it moved. Thank God. But it hurt. I knew I had done damage. I spent the next three days feeling like an idiot. But it also meant I had to focus on getting fit, rather than spend the week feeling sorry for myself over not getting picked.

DECLAN KIDNEY: After the the captain's run in Murrayfield, Paul and Gert came to me. Jerry was a doubt and we'd flown in Bernard Jackman as cover. They said, 'Can we get a hall tonight to do some lineouts?' I said no. Every time you do something there's an opportunity lost to be doing something else. These fellas

will work morning, noon and night and they needed to be fresh. Sometimes your job is to say no – even to intimidating fellas like Paul and Gert.

LES KISS: Scotland's defence coach [Graham Steadman] had worked with our players for the previous three years and over there people were saying: 'Insider knowledge is going to win this.' But the defining thing wasn't about inside knowledge – it was about what this meant to these guys. Then somebody [Sean Lineen, the Glasgow coach] came out and said that said Rog wouldn't tackle a fish supper. To attack players in that fashion is a joke. You don't have to say those things. But I rubbed my hands together because they just don't get it. If that's how they think they'll break a team down then they're kidding themselves.

RONAN O'GARA: I saw that – the Glasgow coach. I would have thought he'd have enough on his plate. If he had studied Munster matches, he would have seen it's been the biggest improvement in my game.

LES KISS: I remember back in autumn Gert and I saying, 'This guy is tough.' We saw him do certain things in training, he's a fighter. The 10–12 channel is the most obvious one to attack. Everyone tried to run at him and he kept putting his body there. I call it fool's gold. I just didn't see the same opportunities as they did – I saw opportunities for us. They can go there, but we love it because he'll stand up and we've got guys around him who'll work within a system and do their job. They just weren't going to yield.

In the first minute we smashed them in a tackle and turned it over, but then the ball bobbled out of our hands and they ran it. Lukey Fitzgerald puts his body on the line and stops the big fella [Simon Danielli]. It's a try-saving moment. Everyone writes, 'Oh, they found space.' They found space because we made the error after the turnover. But the key thing was we saved the situation – we healed the wound. Every system is going to break down somewhere. It can be fatal – or you can find a way to fight your way back.

PAUL O'CONNELL: Ill-discipline at the start cost us and Chris Paterson almost never misses with penalties so we paid a price. We were definitely a bit tentative. We weren't giving the backs much decent ball.

MALACHY CLERKIN, *SUNDAY TRIBUNE:* Rob Kearney, Luke Fitzgerald and Tommy Bowe were all hungry but there was precious little to feed them with, the Scottish defence choking off all roads like they were locking down a city.

HUGH FARRELLY, *IRISH INDEPENDENT:* The scrum was never secure. For the first time this year, Ireland were clearly outmatched in this area.

DENIS LEAMY: In that first half I was carrying a ball off a kick-off and got hit directly on my left shoulder. I had come back from a bad injury to my other shoulder and it felt the same. I'd lost all power, I couldn't move it. I had to go off, for the team's sake.

BRIAN GREEN: Denis was distraught. I went through the tunnel with him, saying, 'Hold on, hold on – it's not like the other shoulder, it's only happened once.' You've got to be positive with these guys. But he was crushed.

PAUL O'CONNELL: We started playing well about ten minutes before half-time – the forwards were getting their hands on the ball a lot more. We started doing the simple things well – getting around the corner, upping the pace. We didn't score a try but we knocked over a few penalties. Then, right before half-time, they nearly scored.

BRIAN O'DRISCOLL: Thom Evans chipped over my head and I was coasting back. I thought Rog would pick it up but it bounced well for Evans and he took off with it. I could see it all unfolding and I saw Tommy coming across.

TOMMY BOWE: The game hadn't been going great for me. I had dropped balls, made mistakes. Ronan had given me an earful.

Evans is a fast guy and he was going at full pelt, so I thought, 'Have a go on the outside here.' I was just about to tackle him when he stepped inside me and all I could get on him then was my left arm. I managed to put him on the deck – I was holding onto him by a finger in the end but I remember the fear, I remember thinking, 'If you don't hold onto this guy, you're not going to be playing next week.' Then all of a sudden I looked and the ball was gone.

Someone had come up behind him and he had offloaded it.

BRIAN O'DRISCOLL: I saw Phil Godman following Evans and I thought, 'I'm probably being a bit lazy here.' I could have worked a little bit harder than I did, but thanks be to God that shock factor kicked in. You forget how tired you are in games when the panic hits and the adrenalin kicks in. Then you're gone. I put the after-burners on and chased after him.

LUKE FITZGERALD: It comes back to margins, doesn't it? If Tommy hadn't made that brilliant tackle on Evans it could have been a different story – we would have been ten points down at half-time. And then Brian came from miles back.

DAVID WALLACE: I was up level with Drico. He turned, I turned. Drico made the tackle while I was still about twenty metres away. It was an unbelievable tackle. It was one of the key moments of the tournament for us – no question – because it was a certain try.

CHAPTER EIGHT

169

NEXT PAGE: Peter Stringer makes the crucial break off a lineout to set up Heaslip for a try

> **I was up level with Drico. He turned, I turned. Drico made the tackle while I was still about twenty metres away. It was an unbelievable tackle.**

LES KISS: So they had their two moments in the sun and the referee was giving them a beautiful ride. Everything was going their way – and then we came out second half and just pumped it.

TOMMY BOWE: We started playing a bit of rugby, we were going at them. We were in their twenty-two when they turned it over and the ball was kicked long and high by Paterson. Normally I would take high balls morning, noon and night. But this one seemed to be that bit far away from me and I thought, 'I'm not going to make this.' I let it bounce – and the bloody thing went straight back towards Paterson, who was charging forward. I went chasing after it and it bounced up again – just as Paterson was arriving for it. He reached out to grab it and sixty thousand people in the crowd and twenty-nine fellas on the pitch probably thought he was gone – under the posts. Nobody knew the sheer horror that was going on in my head: 'Please come back to me! Oh please, ball! Come here to me!' I don't know how, but I got a hand to it and I was able to regather it. I didn't know he was under the posts, until I saw it afterwards. The amount of people who came up to me and said, 'Jesus – I thought Paterson was gone.' Declan told me: 'Do I have to tell you again? Whatever about letting the ball bounce once – don't let it bloody bounce twice.'

PAUL O'CONNELL: We played well in the second half – although not fabulously well. We scored a good try and Strings did brilliantly.

JAMIE HEASLIP: Paulie called a lineout ball off the top on me and I popped it down to Strings. Their 7 [John Barclay] had shot off the back of the lineout – because off the top we had been going straight to Rog the whole game.

PETER STRINGER: The 7 was the last guy at the end of the lineout and he was nearly always marking Rog. I was hoping Rory would throw it to Jamie – because that meant the next guy in would have to lift – and if the 7 shoots off onto Rog there's going to be a gap. If it was thrown to the front, then the guy inside the 7 might not have had any interest in lifting that second pod and he would have been in the way.

I got a good ball off the top from Jamie and had a quick look at Rog. As I glanced back I could see the 7 had no interest in me.

JAMIE HEASLIP: The second I came down I saw Strings take off. It just opened up – the 7 left such a big hole and Strings isn't slow so he went straight through it. I just ran straight up the pitch and he went on this crazy little swervy run.

PETER STRINGER: I could see the defenders closing in around me. I knew I would have to buy a bit of time before anyone got to me because it wasn't really possible to make the line myself, the way the defence was coming over. I wanted to keep them off me for a bit longer, keep them guessing about where they were going to reach me. If it happened again you could do something different. You don't think about where you're going, your body takes over and you just react.

JAMIE HEASLIP: I kept running straight. I thought he didn't hear me because he looked around. I was screaming 'Strings! Strings!' but I thought he didn't hear me. Then he just turned at the last minute and popped it back and I went flying in.

> He reached out to grab it and sixty thousand people in the crowd and twenty-nine fellas on the pitch probably thought he was gone – under the posts.

The reaction I had when I knew I was going to score – there was a lot behind it, a lot of things playing out for me.

BRENDAN FANNING, *SUNDAY INDEPENDENT:* Heaslip could hardly contain himself, so much so that he was ludicrously lax about completing the touchdown. So it was referred upstairs. There's a lesson there for him – not the first tutorial on this subject – and luckily he learned it at no cost.

JAMIE HEASLIP: I had just scored a try in an international which I didn't start – which I'd been dropped for. The reaction I had when I knew I was going to score – there was a lot behind it, a lot of things playing out for me.

LES KISS: I thought we were all over Scotland in the second half. How anyone could say we snatched the victory is beyond me. In the end we won by seven points [22–15]. We could have got more but it's a difficult game over there.

STEPHEN FERRIS: It was one of the games that I enjoyed most and there was a good buzz afterwards, music playing in the changing room. Rala put some Christy Moore on and everyone was getting showered with a smile on their face. Warren Gatland said we were singing and dancing like we'd won the Six Nations. That was nonsense. We knew we had a massive challenge ahead of us, the biggest game of our lives.

DENIS WALSH, *SUNDAY TIMES:* After the match, Declan Kidney was asked if we could talk about Grand Slams now and for once he stumbled over his words. He began to say that it was too soon and then realized that he couldn't put it off any longer. This team can't put it off any longer. Now is the time. This is the chance of a lifetime: for redemption, for fulfilment. At last.

DONNCHA O'CALLAGHAN: It was going to be the game that would define a lot of our careers. We knew if we lost it, we'd be known forever as bottlers. Nobody in the squad was talking about the sixty-one years since Ireland last won a Grand Slam – we were focused on ourselves. We were all watching the England–France game the day after we beat Scotland and somebody asked Jeremy Guscott, 'Who will win next week?' He half laughed and said, 'Wales – Ireland will choke.'

To be fair, when it had come down to it before, we hadn't produced. We had knocked on the door a few times and made a balls of it. And now this was it – nothing less than a must-win game for us. We had to nail it home. It was a game that could scar your career if you lost it.

CHAPTER 9
THIS IS THE DAY

PAUL MCNAUGHTON: Early in the week stuff came out from Warren Gatland about the Welsh players not liking the Irish players. It was Mickey Mouse nonsense. Nobody actually believed it and he didn't do himself any favours, but the press made a big issue out of it. There was this rubbish as well about the Irish players celebrating in the dressing room at Murrayfield until late into the night. If you're going to play the media game with that kind of stuff, then our job is just to tone it down. At a press conference I must have been asked the same question six times. Instead of saying, 'Listen, lads, I've answered the bloody question', I kept answering it. Because I thought they'd make a big deal out of it otherwise.

TOMMY BOWE: I was getting all the stick for it. The boys were saying, 'Jesus, we sent Tommy off to bloody Wales for one year and now all the Welsh boys hate us! They liked us last year, they liked us the year before – but now they all hate the Irish.'

PAUL MCNAUGHTON: Both the Welsh and Irish media had a go at Gatland because clearly his goading of Ireland hadn't worked. We weren't coming back saying, 'Yes – we hate the Welsh as well.' We treated it with the disdain it deserved. They were going at him, so he turned around and said what he said.

GERRY THORNLEY, *IRISH TIMES:* Gatland wondered whether he should 'take a leaf out of Declan Kidney's book'. Implored not to do so by a Welsh journalist, he then added: 'That's probably the way to go in the future, clichés and say nothing.'

PAUL MCNAUGHTON: That's the kind of thing that Declan doesn't get involved

in – personal stuff. Some of the stuff back in the Leinster days was quite personal. Ultimately, he's a private guy. It was a stupid thing for Gatland to say, but it was his last throw of the dice.

LES KISS: Warren was doing what any coach has to do – set the environment as he reads it. The Welsh–Irish thing was more about deflecting the conversation away from Wales and the fact that they didn't get the job done against France. Against Italy it was touch and go for them for a while. So if he allows the conversation to go there, it adds to the pressure. He found a way to shift the focus.

❝ **What Declan doesn't say says volumes in itself. In not responding to Gatland's comments, he said it all.** ❞

The thing some people didn't take into account was that there was a Grand Slam opportunity for Ireland sitting there, a lot of emotion. And the truth is this: what Declan doesn't say says volumes in itself. In not responding to Gatland's comments, he said it all. One of the true arts of coaching is what you leave out.

RONAN O'GARA: During the week I was bouncing ideas off Paulie. Essentially, winning a game of rugby boils down to your forwards. Those boys have to be on top of their game – they are the men who deliver space for you. Paul is a big thinker on the game, which is rare for a forward. He's very strong-willed and strong-minded. Do we argue? Of course. Do we have shouting matches? Yeah. We argue about things like defensive reorganization. He'd want me to move one way and he'd eat the head off me.

'Move in there! Get in there!'

'*You* move! I'm going around here!'

But what's important is team performance – and the way we think about the game is similar.

DECLAN KIDNEY: Wales had to win by thirteen points to take the championship off us. You don't want to put negative thoughts in their head, but we had to be responsible too. If we are down fifteen points with three minutes to go and we get a penalty – you have to kick it to win the championship.

I had to discuss it. Not to put the onus off me and onto them – but I wanted them to have some bit of thought in their heads. I didn't want it to be a spur-of-the-moment decision. I said, 'We're six points down and there are three minutes left. We get a penalty – what do we do?'

BRIAN O'DRISCOLL: Six points, seven points, taking penalties, not taking penalties – all this stuff. The big thing was the penalty at six points down.

RONAN O'GARA: I said, 'There's no way we're kicking a penalty. Deccie says, 'I knew *you'd* take the gamble anyway.'

DECLAN KIDNEY: I knew I would be shot for letting them do it, if it led to a Welsh try under the posts and cost us the championship. You come away with diddlysquat.

But I knew they were going to go for it and I didn't have a problem then, once we had done it in a responsible way. I spoke earlier about the balance between telling them what to do and wanting them to make decisions. That was a decision that could be talked about before the game. But once we talked about it, fine. It's their game, their time in life.

BRIAN O'DRISCOLL: Paulie was being a bit more polite about it to Deccie.

RONAN O'GARA: Paulie has become very good at being diplomatic. But as I keep telling him: 'You can read all the psychology books in the world – but you have an inner switch and you can't do anything about it.' There's only so much he can take – and then he'll snap. Which is great, you know?

PAUL O'CONNELL: These guys make me laugh – Rog talking about me having a switch? He has an *unbelievable* switch.

GEORDAN MURPHY: On the Thursday, me and Donncha staged a sprint race for the management. At first they thought they'd get away with it, then they were whingeing. It was a handicap, so older guys like Rala and Alan Gaffney were running 45m, we had Deccie on 65m and Paul McNaughton on 70m – we thought he'd be faster than he turned out to be because he's an ex-international back. Les was back on 80m and Gert was complaining about dodgy knees. He said

> 6 **Paulie has become very good at being diplomatic. But as I keep telling him, you can read all the psychology books in the world – but you have an inner switch and you can't do anything about it.** 9

he'd have to jog it, so we put him on 55m. They all started giving out then: 'Hold on a minute! I can't be 70 if he's 60, I want to be 65 …' They took off and Deccie was going well but then Gert's competitive streak took over – he forgot about jogging and went for it. Mark Tainton got off to a flyer but it looked a dodgy start. With about ten metres to go Rala was in front …

PADDY 'RALA' O'REILLY: I was going great, so I was. But it was thirty-five years since I ran and the legs went from underneath me. There was two training balls in front of me and I grabbed them and screamed. I could see Ronan O'Gara: 'Rog! Rog! Me legs! I'll never walk again!' The pain was shocking. Willie Bennett and Dave Revins looked after me. And I was winning the fecking race.

GEORDAN MURPHY: Ger Carmody pipped Willie Bennett for the bronze medal after we disqualified Mark for cheating. Deccie was so close to the gold – but Gert claims he just pipped him. I'm still not sure – I want to see the video evidence from Merv.

BRIAN O'DRISCOLL: I was very, very nervous on the Thursday. I'm not usually a nervous person, but I wanted it so badly. Then I had my captain's meeting on the Friday – I always have it at quarter past six. It was fairly stressful through the day and then I sat down, thought about what I was going to say. I've done fifty-six captain's meetings and it's difficult to come up with new things for each one. I can't go in unprepared and just ad lib – I need to have a focal point. As I started writing things down, a calm came over me. It helped me to see things on paper, seeing what we were going to do. I started believing myself what I was writing and that felt good. I was stress-free after that – I went into my captain's meeting completely relaxed. What I said was all about reinforcing belief. Stamping down on *any*, any sign of doubt. Belief, belief, belief.

LUKE FITZGERALD: I was really worried – I had picked up a back injury. I couldn't sit down in the bus all week. It was one of the biggest games you'll ever play and I didn't feel that fit. At the team run I was nearly falling over when I was trying to sidestep. Deccie sat me down the night before the game and calmed me down. I was a bit upset and he spotted it. His man-management skills are top quality.

‘ **As I started writing things down, a calm came over me. It helped me to see things on paper, seeing what we were going to do. I started believing myself what I was writing and that felt good. I was stress-free after that – I went into my captain's meeting completely relaxed.** ’

JAMIE HEASLIP: He's always around, always floating about the team, picking up on things.

DENIS LEAMY: I was in serious pain when I woke up the morning after the Scotland game. I went to get scanned and it was too sore to even touch. I was in very bad form for the day. Brian Green said, 'Tomorrow morning, you've got to come with a different attitude.' So we did two or three sessions on it. For the next five days I was taking the anti-inflams and icing it and he'd take it through a few motions. I did a fitness test the day before the game and felt okay. I told the coaches I was good to go. Gert Smal was questioning me.

'If you had to come on in the first five minutes, would you be okay?'

'Not a bother. No problem.'

It was still sore, but I felt I could manage the pain. These are the things you have to go through. They probably had it in their heads that they wouldn't use me unless they really had to.

TOMMY BOWE: The night before the match we were having a bit of a chat in Rala's room, eating a few Curly Wurlies. Rog was there, Leams, Rory, Paulie, Micko, Paddy. I was having a packet of crisps as well and the boys were saying, 'How do you get away with eating bloody crisps? You're still as skinny as a rat.'

Nobody was too uptight, there was a lot of laughing and joking, people falling

GRAND SLAM

onto the bed and messing up Rala's socks and shorts. I was just about to walk out when I heard this roar from Rala again. The boys grabbed him and we wrapped him up in duvets, bound him and gagged him with duct tape – and carried him out to the lift. It was a glass lift and we sent it all the way down to the lobby. People were standing there waiting and when the doors opened, they stepped back in total shock. By this stage the rest of the team had heard the commotion and everyone was hanging over the balcony.

PADDY 'RALA' O'REILLY: I was sent up and down five or six times. One man waiting for the lift was on a crutch – he let the crutch fall and ran.

Saturday, 21 March 2009

RALA'S THOUGHT OF THE DAY: *Carpe Diem* – Seize the day.

JACK KYLE: Karl Mullen used to say, 'Is nobody going to take this 'oul Grand Slam away from us?' It was a long, long time ago. We had sixty-one years of being the only Grand Slam winners and we'd enjoyed it. But there aren't many of us left and this new generation deserved a Grand Slam.

Neil Hughes, a friend of my son Caleb, said to him, 'I'm going over to Cardiff and I'm taking my father. Why don't you come and take your old man?' We left from Dublin early on Saturday morning, a gorgeous day.

DONNCHA O'CALLAGHAN: That Saturday was hell. I thought we'd never get to half-five.

PAUL O'CONNELL: Donners was suffering but I was fine. I was reading Richard Branson's book, *Losing My Virginity*. The start of it is brilliant, but in the end he starts going on about his charity work. I wanted to read about how he made the money.

GORDON D'ARCY: Normally I get stuck in to my food, but I could hardly eat anything at lunch.

RUTH WOOD-MARTIN, NUTRITIONIST: On a normal day these guys line up for meals and it's demolished. The bigger players go through five or six thousand calories a day. On a match day, they have to force themselves to eat because they know they need it, but it's not enjoyable for them.

SLAM

190

GRAND

‘On a match day, they have to force themselves to eat because they know they need it, but it's not enjoyable for them.’

MARK TAINTON: In the afternoon we played a little handling game, forwards versus backs, with lots of Irish supporters there cheering on the boys. When we got to the ground for the warm-up Rog was kicking straight into the Irish fans and they were boosting and boosting him.

JERRY FLANNERY: I couldn't wait for the whistle. The Welsh like to create one-on-ones, mismatches. They like to isolate players. Our feeling was that we were a team and we weren't going to be broken. There was always going to be a line of green jerseys – no gaps, an unbreakable line.

RONAN O'GARA: Before the match, Gert grabbed me by the jersey. He said, 'You must be physical today.' He threw down a challenge to me. That was fair enough – it's not as if I'm known for my spear-tackling. I could see what it meant because

when he was talking during the week there were tears in his eyes. I like that – it shows he's not just picking up his pay packet. He's concerned and ambitious for us and I was thinking, 'I'd love to produce for this fella.' After that, I was buzzing going out there.

GERT SMAL: I just wanted to give him even more confidence to be physical. Ronan is mentally strong enough to activate himself. It was just a pointer so that when they did come at him – and everyone knew they would – then that seed is planted.

PAUL O'CONNELL: I remember Josh Lewsey telling me that a big part of the game plan at Wasps when they played Munster was 'Get Rog off the pitch.' Target him. That day at Lansdowne Road, he did his hamstring. He could have done it bending over to pick up the ball, but they felt it worked. So we come up against Wales, who have Shaun Edwards and Gatland, and we knew the same thing would be in place. But Donners was at hand to sort it out.

DONNCHA O'CALLAGHAN: I knew they'd have a huge price on Rog's head. They targeted him big-time – and we're a different team without him. I know Ryan Jones from the Lions – real nice guy, no malice in him at all. When I saw him doing it in the first minute I thought, 'If Ryan Jones is thinking of giving Rog a belt, imagine the way the rest of them are thinking.' I probably shouldn't have got involved that early on but I wanted to let him know that I knew what they were at – and they weren't getting away with it.

Playing with Rog is like playing with your sister – you have to mind him.

RONAN O'GARA: They were trying to bash me up, get their heavy traffic running at me. I had a shouting match with a Llanelli fella [Dafydd Jones]. He was genuinely offended with what I came back at him with in the heat of battle. But I was a

‘ **Playing with Rog is like playing with your sister – you have to mind him.** ’

> **No matter how much information you have in your head, when you get out on the pitch that doesn't rule – natural ability rules.**

lot worse three or four years ago – I've copped myself on. Sledging serves no purpose, really. People say, 'Don't let it rattle you.' It doesn't – but there's only so much you can take. The smart fellas will say, 'Turn the other cheek and smile at them.' But I don't know … I actually enjoy a bit of it.

ROB KEARNEY: My back went into spasm in the first minute. I was in a bad, bad way. Had it been any other game I probably would have come off but the occasion was so massive and the atmosphere was so incredible you didn't want to leave. My memory of the game is being in pain throughout it.

MERVYN MURPHY: We did a lot of work in the analysis room on Wales and the players put in a lot of hours. I've huge admiration for the decision-makers – the number 9s, the 10s, the locks who make the lineout calls, the hookers, the captain. That's the measure of a top-class player – how much detail they can take on board without letting it affect their game. Guys like Paul O'Connell and Brian O'Driscoll have so much going through their heads in a massive match like that, a Grand Slam decider, I sometimes wonder how they can even play the game.

BRIAN O'DRISCOLL: No matter how much information you have in your head, when you get out on the pitch that doesn't rule – natural ability rules. Merv knows everything about how the team ticks. He's a massive component to our team, he gives us an edge – but the one thing we have on Merv is that we've played international rugby and it's about instinct. You've got to let it happen.

At times against Wales I could feel the analysis point of view clicking in: 'Gavin Henson is running at me in broken phase. I know he's going to come off his right foot because I've chatted to Merv about it and we've analysed that. I know he has a right-foot chop step – so I can line myself up for the hit.'

They are the minutiae that are essentially the difference in big games, but at the same time it's important not to get bogged down on analysing teams. You've really got to concentrate on yourself and your own performance, no matter what side comes up against you. You have to believe that what you implement yourself determines the outcome of the game, not the way you can defend against someone – because that's a negative thought.

STEPHEN FERRIS: In the first ten minutes I went to dive on a ball and Martyn Williams went to hack it through. He kicked the ball, followed through and hit my right index finger. The bone was shooting out the back of my hand. I shouted over to Paul: 'Paulie – my hand's wrecked!'

JAMIE HEASLIP: It was disgusting – and he wanted to play on. Fez was just walking around with this bone sticking out, saying, 'Come on! Let's get on with it!'

STEPHEN FERRIS: I got back in the defensive line and Paulie shouted over: 'Ref! It's a compound dislocation – you have to stop the game!' Our doctor Mick Webb's first word was 'Jesus!' He tried to get it back in a couple of times but it wasn't slipping in. He was saying, 'Stevie – we've got to get you off.'

CAMERON STEELE: Over the mike Declan heard 'dislocated finger' and couldn't understand why we weren't strapping him up and getting him back on. In that situation the coach is obviously going to freak out – Denis coming on for seventy minutes wasn't the plan, not after his injury. It's hard to explain what a bone sticking through skin looks like to a coach in that pressure cooker. So Stephen had to be dragged off. He could have lost a finger if he'd been allowed to stay on.

'**Fez was just walking around with this bone sticking out, saying, 'Come on! Let's get on with it!'**'

'I got a great lift from the Irish supporters. They were totally outnumbered but I could hear them singing and chanting.'

STEPHEN FERRIS: On my way off Mick had another go and he got it back in. I got it cleaned up and stitched and it looked in pretty good shape but head doctor wouldn't let me continue. He said, 'This isn't your call – it's ours. This is the best decision for you.' In the changing room, I put my head in my hands. A few tears came to my eyes. Then I slapped myself around the back of the head and said, 'Come on – pull yourself together!' I watched the rest of the game biting my fingernails.

LES KISS: Losing Ferris early was a blow, but we had Denis Leamy. So they look up and think, 'Jesus, another monster.'

DENIS LEAMY: I thought it was a blood injury. Ten minutes in, I was wondering where Stephen was. Nobody had told me he wasn't coming back on. I was keeping an eye out for him, but he never came back.

LUKE FITZGERALD: I had been really nervous about how I was going to hold up but when I was out there I enjoyed every moment. Early on I thought I'd got over for a try in the corner. Utter elation. Unbelievable. But then I heard a big 'Ohhhhhhh' from the Irish supporters. I turned around and he had given a forward pass.

MARCUS HORAN: The game plan was – rip into them from the start. I was up against Adam Jones – a heavy man. It was a frustrating game for myself and John, to be honest. We weren't doing anything different, but we got penalized a fair bit. But I got a great lift from the Irish supporters. They were totally outnumbered but I could hear them singing and chanting.

GORDON D'ARCY: I didn't want half-time to come. I just wanted to keep playing, keep running. I remember looking across the field at our line and thinking, 'These guys aren't going to get through.'

JERRY FLANNERY: I got busted in the first half – seven stitches to my eye. Everyone else was going to the dressing room and I had to go off to some doctor's room. Our own doc was with the rest of the lads and this guy came in with a crappy, stripey blazer on him. He was so relaxed, joking with everyone around him. I didn't know anyone there and I was thinking, 'Just get the stitches in and get me the hell out of here. I'm not here for small talk.' I was dying to get into the dressing room.

PAUL O'CONNELL: We went in 6–0 down at half time – six disappointing points for us to give away. But I thought we had been playing quite well – we'd spent a lot of time in their territory. I was happy enough.

RONAN O'GARA: The mood was poor. You're thinking, 'One more score for these guys and we're chasing the game big-time.' But at the same time I was impressed with the mental state of fellas. I didn't see any heads going down. We'd had a lot of possession and nothing to show for it. I said to myself, 'Stick with it, stick with it – this can turn.'

CAMERON STEELE: Rob Kearney's back had been in spasm since the Thursday and at half-time he was in absolute agony. He put a compression strap on but he had no business playing twenty more minutes to be honest. To take to the field for the second half was a really brave act.

TOMMY BOWE: Les Kiss came over to me and said, 'Get your hands on the ball – because they're scared of you when you're running at them.' It was nice to hear that and I thought, 'I've got to get more involved in this game.'

LES KISS: Half-time was special. Brian pulled them into a circle after we'd said our bit. He said he believed 100 per cent in the players. He said: 'I believe in *us*.' That was as special a moment as I've seen in a dressing shed. Going back out

Paul was saying, 'We're unbreakable! We're unbreakable!'

LUKE FITZGERALD: We started well in the second half – had to. Had to score next.
We got down there and the forwards started going at them.

PAUL O'CONNELL: Pick and go, pick and go. Keep hammering away at them. Keep
taking them on up front.

LUKE FITZGERALD: I knew it wasn't going wide. I was in the last ruck. D'Arce was
going mad at me, saying, 'Get out of there!' Tomás fed it back again and I just
latched onto Paulie.

BRIAN O'DRISCOLL: They drove on, they were only a yard and a half, two yards out.
It came back through Paul's legs and I was on it. Fla was with me. I saw the line
and went low. I got it down – but I wasn't sure. It was very close because I lost
control immediately after it hit the line.

   Fla was nodding his head, telling me I'd got it down. In fairness to the referee,
he might have penalized us seventeen times but he was the only one in the ground
who saw that try. Rog knocked over the conversion and from being six points
down we were leading.

*Twenty-three seconds after Stephen Jones restarts the match, Waynes Barnes blows for an
Ireland scrum ten yards inside their own half, dead centre. O'Gara calls the play. The scrum
is solid and as O'Leary finds O'Gara, the Welsh backline shoots forward in a blitz defence.
On the right wing, Tommy Bowe is on the move, looking across at O'Gara as he runs,
waiting for him to pull the trigger.*

'I intended kicking it end over end behind the defence so that it would bounce up, but you never know with a rugby ball.'

RONAN O'GARA: It was quite speculative. There's a small bit of skill involved in it and a fair bit of luck. I intended kicking it end over end behind the defence so that it would bounce up, but you never know with a rugby ball. I put it in space, but it was probably a forty-sixty ball for Tommy.

TOMMY BOWE: I was running straight along the touchline – I was hoping he'd kick it a bit further across the pitch, closer to me. It was a peach of a kick but it went a bit short, further infield. I had to change my line and as I moved inside it bounced straight up – perfect. Shane was chasing back, Gavin was tearing up from full-back and it bounced right in between them. I took it with two hands over my head and Gavin hit me an awful smack in the stomach – he totally winded me. It fell out of my hands but I grabbed it and just went straight under the posts.

The boys jumped on top of me and I couldn't breathe, I had to push them off. I couldn't even celebrate. My mum and brother were right behind the posts and somebody asked her, 'What were you thinking when Tommy scored the try?'

She said, 'I didn't even see it – I had my hands over my eyes.'

PAUL O'CONNELL: Another seven-pointer – massive. But then there was some indiscipline – we gave away six points. I wasn't happy – I had a word – because we didn't need to do it and it put them right back into it.

RONAN O'GARA: Once we got the second try we were flying but we made hard work of it. That's where we need to improve as a team – we should have kicked on and beaten them more.

DONNCHA O'CALLAGHAN: We were winning at the lineout, we were playing all the rugby – and we weren't pulling away. It showed how much of a quality side they were, because they weren't at their best. That game should never have come down to what it did.

JOHN HAYES: They were two points behind when I gave away a penalty out by the halfway line. Next thing I saw Henson coming up to take it. I thought. 'Jesus, this fella has a big boot on him.' I was fair relieved to see that fall short.

RORY BEST: The clock was ticking, over and over. I started thinking, 'Maybe I'm not going to get on here.' Sixty minutes. Sixty-five. Geordan came off the bench. Then me and Peter were told to get ready. No regrets – just get stuck in.

GEORDAN MURPHY: Wales are a dangerous side – when they're chasing a game they're even more dangerous. We were less than ten minutes away from a Grand Slam and we were making a few mistakes. They were throwing everything at us and they have some game-breakers.

CAMERON STEELE: It was seriously physical. With five minutes left Rory Best offloaded from a turnover and Luke kicked upfield, but got hit into touch. He damaged his right collarbone joint. He was hurting, he was in a lot of pain. He wasn't sure if he could carry on – he didn't want to let the team down.

LES KISS: The medics were there, doing what they should. But the timing couldn't have been worse because they were coming hard at us. Mark Tainton was shouting at Cameron, 'He must get up! He's gotta be in there!' Five or six seconds later he didn't seem to be moving, so then I started shouting. *'He has to get up!'*

CAMERON STEELE: It's white noise at that stage, you just really have to do your job and establish if he can continue. We did a quick diagnosis and I said, 'It's not going to get any worse – you're safe to make a hit – get back in.' It wasn't ideal, but he could go back on and give us time to get the sub ready.

LUKE FITZGERALD: I was hoping the play would just pass me by. I ran back on – just as Mike Phillips was breaking through. I thought, 'I can't believe this! This is the worst thing!'

PETER STRINGER: I tried to tackle him but I went too high and he brushed me off and broke away. He was gone.

LUKE FITZGERALD: It was just bodies on the line. It was mayhem. I couldn't lift my arm so I just went in and hit him as hard as I could. He just sat me down – I was a speed bump.

PETER STRINGER: Luke slowed him down and I managed to get back to him.
It's instinct then, it's panic. You don't want to be the one that lets them through.
This time I went for his legs and I got him down.

DECLAN KIDNEY: Which is the most important part of all that – that the physio let
Lukey go back on, that he got his body in the way or that Peter had two cracks
at Phillips?

LES KISS: Shit happens. They got through us. But we found a way. They got a drop
goal from that move, but a three-pointer – not a seven pointer.

RONAN O'GARA: I nearly got a blockdown on Stephen Jones for his drop goal –
I could see it coming. But when I saw that kick going over, something clicked
inside me. I got excited. I started thinking … *You're going to have a kick to win this.
You're going to have one shot at this to win it for Ireland.*

PADDY WALLACE: It got to seventy-five minutes. Seventy-six. I was thinking, 'This
isn't going to happen for me.' And he wasn't going to make a change – until Luke
got injured. Stephen Jones kicked the drop goal and Mervyn Murphy shouted over
to me, 'You're on! You're on!' So I'm just running around like crazy. Because I'm
fresh. Because I'm trying to help everyone.

PAUL O'CONNELL: There were no major tactical thoughts in my head. All I was
thinking was, 'We've just got to get down there and get three points.'

RONAN O'GARA: Poor restart from me. Too far – didn't get enough height on it.
Ball outside the twenty-two. Pass back into it – to Stephen Jones. They never kick
to touch – but he blew it in on the full. I thought, 'They're after miscalculating
here. Big-time.'

MARK TAINTON: Nine times out of ten, their 9 would have box-kicked from where
he was. We'd done the analysis. Nearly always when he receives the ball in that
position, he kicks. But he's feeling pressure. He wants to get rid of the ball.
So he passes to Jones.

DECLAN KIDNEY: Wally put great pressure on Jones. He came from the outside and closed him down ever so slightly. Another of the little things.

MARCUS HORAN: All the way back for our lineout – and for some reason I just knew this was it: all or nothing. It felt right. Everyone seemed focused. All I was thinking of was, 'We're going over for a try here.' I never even thought about a drop goal.

RORY BEST: All I knew was, we had to win this lineout. If Wales turned us over and kicked down the pitch we might not get another chance. Whenever Paul makes a lineout call you never question if it's the right one, because you know he's spent about four hours looking at it that week.

PAUL O'CONNELL: It's a massive tactical battle, the lineout. You're trying to win their ball based on the analysis you've done. You're trying to call your own based on their guess about what you're going to do.

You have to be guessing what they're guessing – so you can sometimes match their guess and make them think, 'Yes, we have it!' There's a little bit of poker in it. You're hoping that they think, for a split-second, that they have it. They go up – and then you win it four feet behind. You need people who know the lineouts inside-out to be able to do that. Everything needs to happen on the button.

I called it on myself. Great throw by Rory, top of the jump. We mauled it. Broke off. Went infield. Picked and went. We made three or four good gains.

MARCUS HORAN: I saw Wally outside and I thought, 'There's no better man to give this to.' I gave him the pass from the base of the ruck. I thought he was going to get over.

RONAN O'GARA: I was back in the pocket. Usually drop goals are instinctive, but this thing was pure torture. I was expecting the ball for ninety seconds before I got it. I was visualizing the ball going straight through the posts. I had so many spots picked out on the hoarding behind the goal. I thought it would never come back to me. It was starting to look like we were going for a try. Wally did his usual and took five men on. I had to move across – I was in the centre now.

SLAM

208

GRAND

Usually drop goals are instinctive, but this thing was pure torture. I was expecting the ball for ninety seconds before I got it.

PADDY WALLACE: When Wally went I was first to arrive at the ruck. I cleaned it out – and then I was just looking around like everybody else, waiting for it to go back to Rog.

RONAN O'GARA: I was roaring at Strings. This was it. There was a perfect second to let it go, before they all rushed up on me. And then Rory gets in the way.

MARK TAINTON: He does fancy himself as a bit of a kicker, Rory. He has a good left peg – very educated. But he needs five or six minutes to do it – not one or two seconds. We were screaming at him. The noise in the box was immense. Seven of us all shouting the same thing.

Get out of the way!

RORY BEST: Suddenly it occurred to me that Rog might be looking for a drop goal here and I'm in the way, so I charged around the corner and Strings threw it back.

MARK TAINTON: It was a great pass onto Ronan's right side. It was bang on the money – there was no adjustment for Rog. If the pass had been on his left, he wouldn't have had time to pull it across. He couldn't look up but he knew they were coming. They looked offside. But was a referee in Cardiff going to give a penalty? Very unlikely. No arm came out.

RONAN O'GARA: It was a sweet pass, but Christ I could feel them. They were all over me. I had to get the ball up quickly. The ball drop was poor. I'm rushing it. It tilts poorly, doesn't sit up. To be honest, it's haunted, it's not charged down. It clears Ryan Jones by inches but I have my chest at the target and the ball goes where your chest points – straight through the posts.

Jesus they were so close – that's a charge-down nine times out of ten. It was one of those things where you think, 'Today's our day.' I'm a believer in that.

DONNCHA O'CALLAGHAN: After Wales got their drop goal someone went down and their physio came on. They were letting us think about it: 'You've been winning this match and now you're losing it.' So once Rog scored I did the same to them. Stephen Jones was abusing me: 'Get out of the way!' I told Wayne Barnes, 'You allowed them to get attention when they scored – I'm asking for the same now.'

Hand on heart, there was nothing wrong with me. But I thought, 'Let them think about this now – us being two points clear and them needing to score.' I thought it might give them a little seed of doubt.

DECLAN KIDNEY: They kicked off and we managed to deal with it alright. Rog did the right thing, putting it down the middle of the field and keeping them back in their own half. Wally had a big tackle on Shane Williams – his third big play in the last few minutes. We were doing okay. Our line was holding. And then ...

PADDY WALLACE: They had the ball in midfield and I came straight through the gate. As they tried to clean me out they shifted me to the side and I could see the ball carrier [Alun-Wyn Jones] at my feet. I thought, 'I've got a chance to poach the ball here.' I was straight on it – it was totally instinctive. I stayed on my feet. I grabbed it and let it go through my legs. Came up. Looked across. Saw his bloody arm going up.

STEPHEN FERRIS: I probably would have done the same thing, tried to steal the ball. It was there to have a go at. The two guys coming in missed Paddy – they didn't totally clean him out. But there were two of them. You can't argue that. So that makes it a ruck.

DENIS LEAMY: I was right beside Paddy. I was conscious that the ref might look to give them an opportunity and I shouted, 'Leave it!' But it happened so quickly.

RORY BEST: I still admire the way he went for it. Someone eventually was going to have to take a bit of a risk to get the ball back for us because they were edging

Laws of Rugby Union: 16.4 (b) Players must not handle the ball in a ruck. Penalty: penalty kick.

their way up the field. They could have kept going and got a penalty closer to the posts. Nobody knows what might have happened.

PADDY WALLACE: You don't give the referee a decision to make. There's no point in looking at the what-ifs. I shouldn't have given him a chance to make a decision. I will never try and justify it. It was the wrong decision and a stupid one.

RONAN O'GARA: I was standing right beside Paddy. The first person he saw when the penalty was given was me. And he was saying, 'What have I done? No!' I couldn't say anything. I couldn't believe it.

PADDY WALLACE: I'm numb. It kicks in straight away, the significance. I look at where we are on the pitch. I know it's within his range. I'm in shock. I've been in a car crash before – it was a similar feeling. Your body tenses and numbs up and you're not aware of anything. It's a surreal feeling – but straight away I'm completely aware of the significance of it.

I walk back on my own. If there's anyone alongside me I don't see them. I'm in my own world. I reach the posts. I look back down the pitch towards Stephen Jones and the clock is behind him. Just as I look up it goes to eighty minutes. That's when I think, 'When he kicks this we have no chance to score again.'

LES KISS: I truly believed that for a kick in the last minute, the attritional brutality of the game might take the legs out of him. The will of the boys still existed then. They were standing up to him and saying, 'Prove it.' They still were having an impact.

DONNCHA O'CALLAGHAN: I was given a role by Paulie – to make sure he didn't claim an extra few feet, even a few inches. I was standing there, pointing, telling the ref, 'I know where that mark is.' I remember praying as he lined it up …

If this is to be for us, it's up to you now.

I looked at the clock and thought, 'This is all over – there's nothing we can do here.' In my head I was saying, 'God grant me the serenity to accept the things I cannot change …'

MARCUS HORAN: I pray before the games. When I got married, the priest said to me, 'When you're going out on the pitch, bless yourself.' That year we won the Heineken Cup and I haven't stopped since. I walked back ten yards from the ball and looked up at the heavens. It was good that the roof was open …

Please don't do this to us. This is cruel. Help us here.

BRIAN O'DRISCOLL: I was absolutely certain that Stephen Jones was going to knock it over. I had no doubt. As I was walking back, flashes went through my head …

This is so unjust. This is so wrong. We deserve this moment. We deserve this Grand Slam.

PAUL O'CONNELL: I just put my head in my hands. All I was thinking was, 'It's over. It's gone. Gone.' Before the game I had believed resolutely – 100 per cent – that we were going to win. So that penalty was a massive shock to my system. I looked at him as he went to strike it. Then I looked away.

LES KISS: There was disbelief in the box. There was shock. But the reality is, it's still a hard kick. Even so, I couldn't bear to sit down and watch it. Alan Gaffney and I got up from our seats. We were going to stand up at the back of the box, but straight away Declan was saying, 'Sit down!' He was right. The game wasn't finished.

DECLAN KIDNEY: Once a teacher, always a teacher.

ALAN GAFFNEY: By the time the camera panned to us, we were back in our seats and looking composed. Or at least that might have been how it looked to people watching on television. Inside, we were a long way from composed. It was sixty

seconds of absolute bloody torment. I thought it was gone. At that stage I was thinking, 'Well, at least we've won the Six Nations.' That would have been an achievement – but in reality it would have been seen as a failure.

JACK KYLE: I turned to Caleb and said, 'Don't tell me Ireland are going to be thwarted again.' He said, 'He's going to kick this. We're going to lose again, Dad.' We could hardly bear to watch it.

MARK TAINTON: His legs were getting tired. To kick the ball fifty metres in the last minute with the pressure on him, to generate that leg power – that was going to be a big, big ask. He's very accurate. He's a fantastic player. But he's not the longest kicker.

PADDY WALLACE: Jesus, I'm getting nervous even just recounting it now. I turned around and before I knew it he was lined up and moving towards the ball. It seemed sudden to me. I was thinking, 'He's taking this a bit quickly – what's he rushing for?'

GEORDAN MURPHY: Under the posts we were saying, 'Can we lift someone here to stop it going over?' But they've changed the rules. We were still talking about it when all of a sudden he stepped up and hit it. I was underneath the black dot and it was coming straight at me, on target.

PADDY WALLACE: As soon as he kicked it I thought it was spinning quite hard. As a kicker you don't want too many revolutions on the ball because energy is taken out of it and it doesn't travel as far.

RONAN O'GARA: I was to the right of the posts. I could see it was dropping short and I got excited – I got attracted to the ball. It's really the full-back's ball and Geordan was right under it – but I was dying to boss the situation.

GEORDAN MURPHY: After two seconds of flight I thought, 'That's not going to make it.' Generally if the full-back calls for it, it's his. I called for it.
   'My ball!'

It's really the full-back's ball and Geordan was right under it – but I was dying to boss the situation.

Rog was going, 'No! Mine! My ball!' That caused a little bit of panic and we screamed at each other once or twice. I roared a little bit more violently than him.

RONAN O'GARA: Just at the last second I got out of the way – I could have caused a bloody knock-on. Geordan was very composed. You felt secure that he was your last man.

GEORDAN MURPHY: I didn't know how much was left on the clock but I knew there was safety in the in-goal area. I could waste time in there – as long as I caught it with my foot inside. I tried to keep my right foot there as I went to catch it. I turned around and looked at the touch judge and said, 'I was inside! I was inside!' He nodded.

PADDY WALLACE: It flew over my head but it was dying fast and I knew it was short. I saw Geordan take it and I put my hands on my head and turned away. At that moment, what I felt was pure relief – indescribable relief. When I looked up again O'Connell was charging up the pitch with this mad stride. He looked like a demented horse.

PAUL O'CONNELL: As soon as Geordie caught it, I looked straight up and saw the numbers were in red. And in fairness, Geordie is the man you want there – he knows all those rules.

BRIAN O'DRISCOLL: I saw Paulie charging off. I thought, 'Where is he going?'

GEORDAN MURPHY: I wanted to kill more time, so I started running for the corner flag. If there was still time left I would have run back again. Until they caught me and forced me to touch it down.

BRIAN O'DRISCOLL: Geordie wasn't sure about the eighty minutes. I knew exactly. I started running after him shouting, 'Kick it into the stand!'

GEORDAN MURPHY: The Welsh players weren't even chasing. I knew it was done and dusted. As soon as I touched it down, the ball's dead, over. Pure excitement took over – I blasted it into the stand.

PAUL O'CONNELL: I had imagined what I would do if we won, thought about how I would react at the moment the whistle sounded. I thought I'd be very calm. But I ran off, I went mad. I don't know what I was doing, I don't know what came over me. But I thought it was gone – and it went from that feeling of total despair to, 'We have a Grand Slam.'

RORY BEST: I've never seen a man so happy. Paul was sprinting towards me and I was thinking, 'Is he going to plough into me here?' But to see what it meant to someone who has achieved as much in the game as he has – that rammed it home for me.

DECLAN KIDNEY: I put my head down and there were people everywhere. It was brilliant.

LES KISS: We had a big hug – it was a pretty special moment. How do you explain the feeling in the lift going down to the pitch? It wasn't relief, nowhere near.

> **More than anyone I felt for Shaggy [Shane Horgan]. For a guy to have played ten years and not to have been part of a Grand Slam-winning team – I would have loved that moment with him.**

We were way past that. To me it was more a sense of real profound achievement and satisfaction among us as a group of coaches.

GERT SMAL: It was good to know that the time that you invested was all worthwhile. Sometimes you do the same amount of work but you don't get the result.

BRIAN O'DRISCOLL: It felt ... weird. It wasn't the elation that I would have felt had there not been that kick. I was so stressed – massive stress. I couldn't get over that emotion for a while. But I remember feeling ... just so grateful. You could name a lot of guys who missed out on that moment but more than anyone I felt for Shaggy [Shane Horgan]. For a guy to have played ten years and not to have been part of a Grand Slam-winning team – I would have loved that moment with him.

Through rugby you work with people and develop friendships and then they finish and you realize they were just colleagues. Shaggy will always be a friend.

A couple of months later, when we won the Heineken Cup, I knew how much it meant to him. As chuffed as I was for myself, I was more chuffed for him and his family. Those memories can't be bought.

JACK KYLE: After the game, somebody took me down from the stand and I met Brian O'Driscoll. Words were unnecessary, really. He was just so happy. Somebody gave me a copy of the photograph of myself with Brian. I'm so delighted to have it.

DONNCHA O'CALLAGHAN: It meant the world to me, but I took no satisfaction from the way we won it. I would rather have been camped on our own line, defending like dogs. I didn't want to celebrate Stephen Jones missing a kick.

PAUL O'CONNELL: In fairness to Rog, I never even thought of Stephen Jones. I hadn't stopped celebrating and Rog had already swapped jerseys with him. That was a touch of class.

PADDY 'RALA' O'REILLY: When the final whistle went I put my hands up to my face, I couldn't believe what the lads had achieved. I went back into the changing room. I'd never felt that emotion before. I was in a different world, a trance. I sat down and put on Christy. There was no one else there, they were all out on the field. I was trying to imagine them being there. It was so tense before they went out – I don't know how they do it. Gerard [Carmody] came in and said, 'Come on, get back out there – we've waited long enough for this.'

PADDY WALLACE: Donncha was the first person to come up to me after the match and say, 'Jesus, Paddy, thank God you gave away that penalty – otherwise I would have got the blame.' The boys joked about it. Every time Ronan looked at me he raised his arm in slow motion and whistled. They were trying to cheer me up – and coming from your fellow professionals it does help. At the end of the day, those are the guys that matter. And those are the guys I would have been most disappointed for had it been different.

I knew how much it meant for us as a squad. I knew the work that had been put in. The blood that was spilled. The desperate longing of some great players to win a Grand Slam. And if it wasn't for two metres of distance, all that would have been taken away. The distance between the kick going over and falling short. And I would have had to walk into that dressing room. I would have had to face the nightmare of that experience. Of looking at my teammates – knowing what it had cost them.

It was hard not to think of what might have been had the kick gone over, of how my life would have changed. I had sleepless nights after it, to be honest. Things started going through my head – what might have been. I'm back on the pitch in Cardiff, watching the ball go over. The thousands of people who were smiling and cheering us in Dawson Street – their joy becomes bitter disappointment and anger at me for giving away the penalty.

I think I had to go through that, because of the magnitude of what happened. It was part of the process of eventually being able to sit back and enjoy it,

LEFT: O'Driscoll greets Jack Kyle, captain of the last Irish team to win the Grand slam, in 1948

knowing that over five matches I contributed to us winning a Grand Slam. The boys gave me their support and Declan gave me his. He was very good about it. That was important for me.

JAMIE HEASLIP: Back in the changing room, you couldn't talk to Paddy. He didn't know what to do with himself. But the thing is, I gave away six points in that game – two penalties that were kicked. I said to him, 'Mate, had I not given those six points away we would have won easily. Your penalty wouldn't have mattered.'

ALAN GAFFNEY: Paddy was shellshocked, he was down in himself. I walked straight over to him.

'Congratulations, Paddy – that was brilliant.'

'What are you talking about?'

'Mate, that was a fantastic technical play. If they had worked another ten metres up the pitch, who knows what would have happened? You must have decided that he couldn't kick it from there, right?'

He smiled – and it was nice to see that smile. Because Paddy had a lot to do with us winning that Grand Slam, he played a big part. And truth is that if that penalty had not been given, no one has a clue what might have happened. It could have been anything.

PAUL O'CONNELL: As soon as the penalty didn't go over, it should have been out of his head. It might bug you a little bit, but he'd done too much to worry about one penalty.

RONAN O'GARA: We had never been sure about what winning a Grand Slam meant. None of us had a clue about how we would feel until we actually won the thing. The feeling in the dressing room was one of unbelievable satisfaction. Did it drop into my head about the Munster fellas not delivering for Ireland? I sat back and smiled to myself. I think that was something that needed to be put right – and I'd like to think it was put right. To be honest, that was a source of motivation to me.

MARCUS HORAN: Everyone needed those few minutes on their own to take it all in. I looked over at Kearns and winked. In a moment like that, you don't have to say

anything. We both knew the Enfield camp was a big deal. What he said could have been the difference – I really felt it did affect a lot of what happened. Later on I said it to him: 'Don't underestimate what you did.'

GORDON D'ARCY: So many people have told me where they were, what they were doing when we won – they were arm in arm, jumping around the place, running out onto the streets where they live, kissing strange men. Everybody has their own memory of where they were.

DR GARY O'DRISCOLL: Halfway through the Six Nations I was offered a job by Arsenal as club doctor. I'd been involved with Ireland for ten years – and when the lads finally won a Grand Slam I wasn't there. It was awful to miss it, it was horrible. We were playing up at Newcastle that day and I told them, 'Please – nobody say anything about the rugby.' But no one did, because no one cared.

I turned my mobile off and we got back to London around 1 a.m. I went to

my hotel and sat on the bed with my laptop, watching the match from the start on BBC iPlayer. I was shouting at the screen. It was a very strange feeling. I was tempted to fast-forward it to the end, but I didn't. I can't tell you how happy I was when they won. By that stage it was three in the morning and I just felt quiet pride and satisfaction. I knew, more than a lot of people, what it meant to them. They would have known it wasn't just about this season. Looking back on it, so many people made it happen, including Eddie, Girvan Dempsey, Shane Horgan, Malcolm O'Kelly, Denis Hickie – many, many people contributed to this. And I thought, 'God, I'd love to be there with the lads.'

Sitting there in my hotel, I could imagine the dressing room in Cardiff. They wouldn't have been going mental – they would have been just sitting there. Proud.

LES KISS: Back into the dressing shed, I saw Declan sitting on his own, sucking it all in. I was the last to leave, other than him. I thought, 'I'll leave him. Leave him have the moment.'

DECLAN KIDNEY: Every so often you find yourself in a place – a happy place – where you don't have to say anything. Not many people get to a place like that. I suppose my only words for it are that your aim is to be able to sit in the dressing room afterwards and look at one another and just nod. That's all. And I think the players will have that for the rest of their lives.

TOP LEFT: Back row: Ger Carmody, Les Kiss, Cameron Steele, Dr Michael Webb; middle row: Karl Richardson, Paul Pook, Alan Gaffney, Declan Kidney, Gert Smal, Mervyn Murphy; front row: Paul McNaughton, Willie Bennett, David Revins, Mark Tainton, Eoin Toolin, Brian Green
BELOW LEFT: Prince William shares a laugh with Heaslip, O'Leary, O'Gara and O'Driscoll

'Every so often you find yourself
in a place - a happy place - where
you don't have to say anything.'

CHAPTER 10
SHINING LIKE THE DIAMONDS

TOMMY BOWE: At the end of the Six Nations in 2008 we had a sing-song. We were trying to drown our sorrows after England beat us at Twickenham and Denis Leamy belted out this song:

'What about her eyes? Her eyes they shone like the diamonds …'

Well, I thought this was the best song I'd ever heard in my life. I was sitting there thinking, 'That is a tune and a half!'At breakfast the following morning all the girlfriends and wives were having a nice little chat and I was singing away on my own.

'What about her eyes?!'

So for the summer tour and through the Six Nations – when we were on the bus or out somewhere – Tomás O'Leary and myself would be giving it a lash. When you shout 'What about her eyes?', everybody sings the chorus louder again.

MARCUS HORAN: He'd let it rip and everyone would join in. They'd give it holly.

TOMMY BOWE: The day after we beat Wales, we came back to Dublin and this massive crowd was waiting for us. The TV cameras were there and your man Des [Cahill] said, 'We'll get a song from Tommy here.'

I was going, 'Yeah, right – obviously not.' But the boys were pushing me out and I had this big dopey grin on my face, a big gappy smile on me. Still in great form from the night before and not really realizing the magnitude of what I'm about to do. But I was sure they wouldn't let me down that much – leave me out on my own. Who'd be harsh enough to do that to me?

TEN

233

CHAPTER

LEFT: O'Driscoll with his girlfriend Amy Huberman, in his hotel room in Cardiff

I let it out – the first verse. It didn't go well at all. But I was sure when I did the 'What about her eyes?' part the guys would be with me. I turned around and half of them don't know whether to fall on the ground laughing and the other half looked like they were going to have a heart attack from the shock of what was happening.

Somebody said, 'You're on television!' At that stage I thought, 'Jesus – I don't know any of the other words!' Des pulled me over then. He said, 'What about that try?' I didn't want to talk about the try, I wanted to get off the stage. A few of the guys were trying to console me – 'It wasn't *that* bad – you didn't make *that* big an idiot of yourself.' Ah sure, at that stage what can you do but enjoy it?

PADDY 'RALA' O'REILLY: That night back in the Killiney Castle, they got me up to say a few words. Everyone was there and I wasn't expecting to have to say anything. I said, 'I immediately think of all the boys who haven't got a Grand Slam. Obviously there's too many to mention. I wouldn't even begin to mention anybody ...'

And then the next sentence, it just came out ... 'People like the Claw.' That brought the house down.

I didn't know I was going to get a medal – I was so thrilled with the whole thing. I think everyone in Inishbofin and Renvyle watched the match. It was their team that won it – the Irish team. So I was delighted for them, all those people.

MARCUS HORAN: A few of the lads started exiting the hotel and there were texts coming back saying they were in the pub up the road, The Druid's Chair. I eventually got up there with Dave Wallace and one of our masseurs, Mocky Regan, got out the guitar. The place had been deserted and now it was packed to the rafters. Locals came in from everywhere. Drink was flowing. Songs were being sung. Nearly the whole squad was there. It's nice to have memories like that, to share a drink with the lads and a bit of a sing-song. Christy would have been proud of us.

It had to end when the youngfellas wanted to go to town and get to the nightclubs. You see the difference in lads. Some of us would have been happy to sit in the pub all night, to have the chat and sing the songs. But you could see a few lads sitting at the edge of the circle, itching to go. You can't fault that either. Everyone has their own thing.

JAMIE HEASLIP: The first thing Paulie said to me when I walked into the pub was, 'What the *hell* are you wearing?'

LUKE FITZGERALD: Paulie just has no dress sense.

DONNCHA O'CALLAGHAN: Paulie would be keen on big guys' fashion. He'll say, 'Where did you get those jeans?' But the lads are right – his dress sense is boring. A nice little polo shirt, a pair of brown shoes, never any bit adventurous. God love him, he's ginger – he can't wear anything. Well, he *was* ginger I should say. Paulie might have slagged Jamie, but he was probably thinking to himself, 'Am I brave enough to wear something like that?'

LUKE FITZGERALD: In fairness to Paulie, it *was* dodgy.

JAMIE HEASLIP: Hey, come on! Don't knock me style here! What are you saying?

LUKE FITZGERALD: I'm saying it was a bold move. I liked it, but it was dodgy.

ROB KEARNEY: It was a grey cardigan, with ah … ah …

JAMIE HEASLIP: It wasn't a cardigan!

MARCUS HORAN: It was a cardigan. Jamie's wearing cardigans. Even John Hayes doesn't wear cardigans.

LUKE FITZGERALD: It was a blazer.

JAMIE HEASLIP: But it wasn't even a blazer …

GORDON D'ARCY: It was Hugo, was it?

JAMIE HEASLIP: No, it wasn't. D'Arce only deals in Hugo. And don't get him started. He's another guy that abused me for the night.

ROB KEARNEY: In fairness to D'Arce, he dresses really well.

LUKE FITZGERALD: It's all free, in fairness …

ALAN ENGLISH: Just for accuracy, can you describe your outfit on the night?

JAMIE HEASLIP: My *outfit?!* It was like … It was kind of … It was a blazer, but it wasn't a blazer. Put it that way.

ROB KEARNEY: It was out there. It was a cotton blazer.

LUKE FITZGERALD: A cream, cotton blazer.

I have a small bit of envy for Lukie and Kearns and the other younger boys who have a Slam under their belts, because it relaxes you.

JAMIE HEASLIP: No! Don't say cotton blazer! It was just … Oh Christ, how would you describe it?

PAUL O'CONNELL: It was a grey cotton tracksuit-type material but in the shape of a suit jacket – with massive stitching on.

LUKE FITZGERALD: It was definitely dodgy.

ROB KEARNEY: I remember the ride in with Paulie. Lukie drove us all into town.

JAMIE HEASLIP: Ah that was brilliant craic! The lads in the back going mad! Paulie was going, 'It's like being with soccer players!'

LUKE FITZGERALD: We had all the Eighties tunes. A bit of Bruce Springsteen, a bit of Tina Turner. Phil Collins in there as well. Paulie was loving it.

PAUL O'CONNELL: Everyone is looking for why we won it – they want a golden reason. But there are probably a hundred little reasons. And a lot of it was experience. We'd had some very good times and some very bad times. Eventually, you find yourself doing the right thing at the right time and you don't know why.

But now this is where it gets most challenging. This is when it's hardest. Going on will be tough. The experience will be great for us, but we've got to make sure we kick on. There are tough times ahead.

BRIAN O'DRISCOLL: If that kick had gone over in Cardiff, nobody would have talked about the Enfield factor – so it just shows the margins are so minute. Once you

GRAND SLAM

get a taste of success, you get very selfish. You want more and more. I remember seeing Ryan Giggs chatting to Cristiano Ronaldo at the European Cup final when United won it [in 2008]. Maybe I'm way off, but I thought he was saying, 'This can be one of many – but you have to want it.'

DECLAN KIDNEY: We all know there are multiple areas we need to improve on. It's my job to know what steps to make at what particular time, to get us to where we want to go. I'm absolutely certain that nobody in the group wants to stay where we are now either.

GERT SMAL: What we came up with for the Six Nations was what worked for us as coaches and for them as players. I don't want to create unrealistic expectations, but it was a long way short of our capacity.

It's down to everybody – the coaches here, in the provinces and in the clubs – to make sure there's a conveyor belt of players coming through. Irish rugby is in a very good place, but I'm still not satisfied. Never just be satisfied with where you are. Enjoy the good times – but see if you can have better times.

LES KISS: Just at the end of this campaign Rob said something that was quite poignant: 'When I was looking up I was seeing a friend next to me, not just a colleague.' Vital, isn't it? And that wraps it up in a lot of ways.

The world moves on. The Grand Slam sits in the right place – kids all over Ireland having their picture taken with the trophy. And if there's another John Hayes there, or another Drico, then that's what it's about.

BRIAN O'DRISCOLL: I've done ten years of this. I'm in the winter of my career and I'm not regretful, because it's getting harder and harder. But I have a small bit of envy for Lukie and Kearns and the other younger boys who have a Slam under their belts, because it relaxes you. I have taken massive satisfaction from being a Grand Slam winner – it's hard to describe just how much, after all these years. But if you think you're the business, that's the end of you. And why would you achieve something special and then go through the motions, accept mediocrity? I can't imagine it.

'Going on will be tough. The experience will be great for us, but we've got to make sure we kick on.'

CHAMPIONS
A PORTRAIT
GALLERY

TOMMY BOWE

RORY BEST

STEPHEN FERRIS

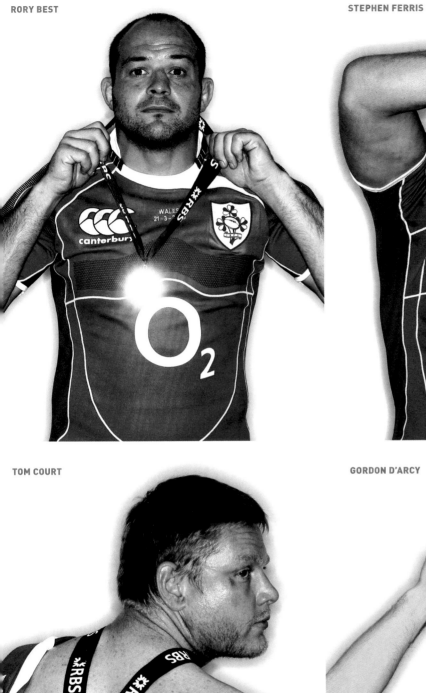

TOM COURT

GORDON D'ARCY

JAMIE HEASLIP

ROB KEARNEY

DENIS LEAMY

GEORDAN MURPHY

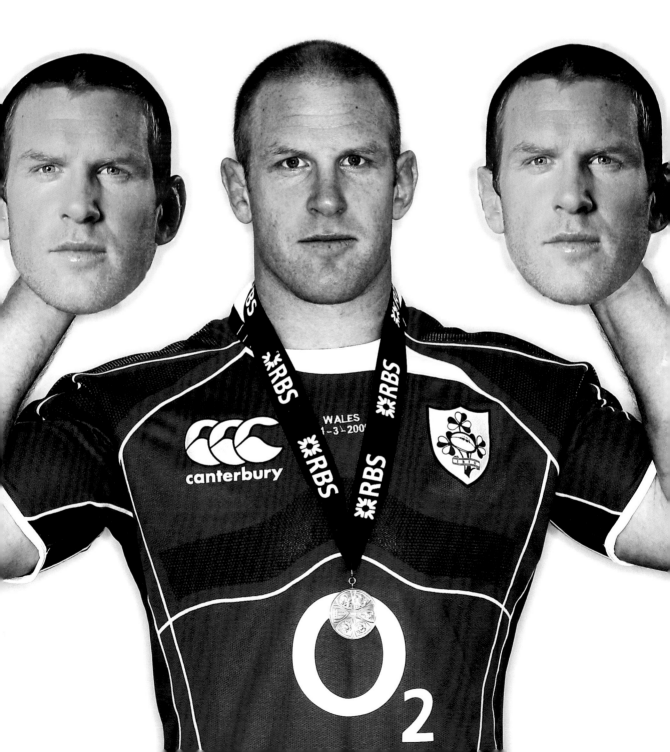

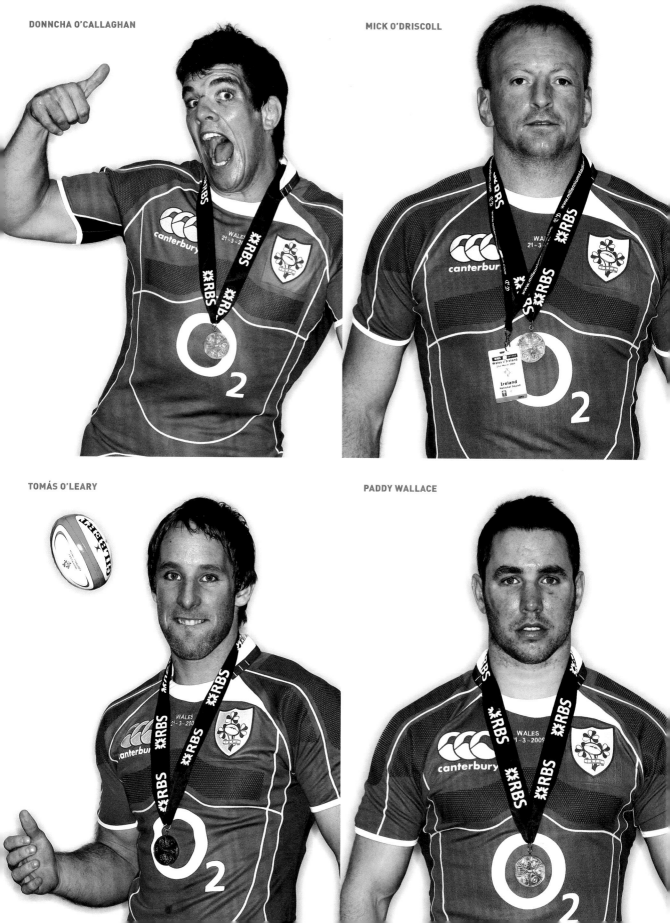

DONNCHA O'CALLAGHAN

MICK O'DRISCOLL

TOMÁS O'LEARY

PADDY WALLACE

PETER STRINGER

ACKNOWLEDGEMENTS

This idea for this book was prompted by the thrilling manner of Ireland's victory against France in their opening Six Nations match in February; six weeks later I found myself at the Fitzpatrick Castle Hotel in Killiney, Co. Dublin, as the players stepped off the bus and were applauded into the foyer as Grand Slam winners. The book got off to a good start, largely thanks to the IRFU's communications and media manager Karl Richardson, and I thank Karl for his help throughout the whole process. Over the next few months I spoke at length to players, coaches and other key personnel in the Ireland set-up and thoroughly enjoyed every conversation. This is their story, their book – and all of them have my gratitude for their honesty, good humour and patience. I would particularly like to thank Declan Kidney and Paul McNaughton for trusting me to tell the story of this team, and I hope I have gone some way towards doing it justice. It was a genuine privilege to be given the opportunity.

As anyone who knows anything about sports journalism in Ireland knows, Billy Stickland is a class act whose photographs elevate the words they accompany. Billy's wonderful pictures – and those of other fine photographers at the Inpho agency – make this great Irish sports story all the more vivid in the telling.

At Penguin Ireland managing director Michael McLoughlin and editor Brendan Barrington were a pleasure to work with and firmly focused on producing a book worthy of the team's historic achievement.

I'd also like to thank my brother Tom for his encouraging words, and for facilitating my own brand of video analysis I'm grateful to my friend and neighbour in Castleconnell, Liam O'Gorman. Thanks also to Padraig Power and Gerard Carmody at the IRFU for their help.

Books are hard on family life and with so many people to interview, meeting the deadline for this one was a challenge I could never have risen to without the love and support of my wife Anne and our children Aisling, Holly and Jack. I can't thank them enough.

ALAN ENGLISH

PHOTO CREDITS